MIGHTY
~ SPICE ~
EXPRESS
COOKBOOK

MIGHTY ~SPICE~ EXPRESS

COOKBOOK

FAST, FRESH AND FULL-ON FLAVOURS
FROM STREET FOODS TO THE SPECTACULAR

JOHN GREGORY-SMITH

DUNCAN BAIRD PUBLISHERS

LONDON

DEDICATION
Sal and Al – I love you!

Mighty Spice Express Cookbook
John Gregory-Smith

First published in the United Kingdom and Ireland
in 2013 by Duncan Baird Publishers, an imprint of
Watkins Publishing Limited
Sixth Floor
75 Wells Street
London W1T 3QH

A member of Osprey Group

Managing Editor: Grace Cheetham
Editor: Jan Cutler
Art Direction and Design: Manisha Patel
Production: Uzma Taj
Commissioned Photography: William Lingwood
Food Stylist: Aya Nishimura
Prop Stylist: Wei Tang

A CIP record for this book is available from the
British Library

ISBN: 978-1-84899-108-8

10 9 8 7 6 5 4 3 2 1

Typeset in Chaparral Pro and LD Bohemian Filigree
Colour reproduction by PDQ, UK
Printed in China

Publisher's note While every care has been taken
in compiling the recipes for this book, Watkins
Publishing Limited, or any other persons who have
been involved in working on this publication, cannot
accept responsibility for any errors or omissions,
inadvertent or not, that may be found in the recipes
or text, nor for any problems that may arise as a
result of preparing one of these recipes. If you are
pregnant or breastfeeding or have any special dietary
requirements or medical conditions, it is advisable to
consult a medical professional before following any
of the recipes contained in this book. Ill or elderly
people, babies, young children and women who
are pregnant or breastfeeding should avoid recipes
containing raw meat or fish or uncooked eggs.

Notes on the recipes Unless otherwise stated:
• Use free-range eggs and poultry
• Use medium eggs, fruit and vegetables
• Use fresh ingredients, including herbs and chillies
• Wash all meat, fish and poultry, and all unpeeled
  vegetables and fruits (apart from mushrooms),
  as well as herbs and salads, and wipe mushrooms
  before preparation
• Do not mix metric and imperial measurements
• 1 tsp = 5ml   1 tbsp = 15ml   1 cup = 250ml

CONTENTS

INTRODUCTION

Food, recipes, cooking, spices and eating are my life, so when my publisher asked me to follow up my first book, *Mighty Spice Cookbook*, I was thrilled. I had already been working on new recipes, so it was a great time to pop the question.

The *Mighty Spice Cookbook* set out to show everyone how simple it was to cook with spices. I never used more than five spices in each recipe and I kept the ingredients supermarket friendly. It made sense that the next step would be to show everyone how fast it is to cook with spices, whatever the occasion. *Mighty Spice Express* was born, and we started putting ideas down. I always like to introduce new recipes and flavours, so I travel abroad for my research. I carefully chose the countries to visit that would give me the most inspiration for express cooking.

'Express' obviously meant street food, and this has been a real inspiration for the book. Street food shows the best a place has to offer and a snapshot of what's hot right now. It is always served fast and furious, and can be hot or cold, savoury or sweet. But, guaranteed, it will be tasty, fresh and cooked to perfection. Quite simply, if the food doesn't cut the mustard it won't be there the following morning.

DUCKING AND DIVING IN FEZ

Mighty Spice Express took me to the stunning city of Fez in Morocco, which has the oldest working *medina* – or old part of the city – in the world. This means a vast expanse of car-free city where people live and trade. The buildings are packed so tightly together that most of the streets are actually narrow passages supported by huge wooden struts, which are best navigated by frequent ducking – Bilbo Baggins and co. would have been perfectly at home.

To an outsider, the city is a maze, and one that needs a guide. Luckily, I had the best in Gail Leonard. Gail organized street-food tours of fabulous Fez and we met one cold January morning by the magnificent Blue Gate. After coffee, we stopped for a cheeky sweetbread sandwich – fried sweetbreads that were served in a roll with spices and finely chopped onions. It was delicious and, strangely, it worked as a great pick-me-up first thing in the morning. It was also the inspiration for my Blue Gate Fez Sandwich in the Mighty Bites chapter.

The natural slope of the ancient city took us south. We wound through narrow passages lit by hazy shafts of light and emerged on to one of the main market streets in Fez. Chickens clucked while waiting for someone's pot, alongside camel heads, spices, herbs, beautiful juicy strawberries, olives, nuts, harissa paste and a wonderful little stall that sold *bessara*. *Bessara* is a breakfast soup made from broad beans. It's rich and thick and perfect for keeping hungry workers full until lunchtime. My bowl was seasoned heavily with chilli and cumin and tasted utterly sublime.

SPECIALITIES FROM THE SEA AT ESSAOUIRA

After Fez I took the train south to the remarkable coastal town of Essaouira. There are times when my job is unbelievable, and this was one of them. I arrived at this magical place and went for a long run along the beach. Kite surfers took off in the sparkling waters around me, horses galloped along the shore and the whole time the setting sun framed the walled city like a movie. I even made some new friends of the canine variety, who followed me all the way back to my hotel. This became slightly awkward when I had to navigate through the fashionable cafés of the town, red faced, sweating and trailed by stray dogs.

Mighty Spice Express is about making any meal occasion fast. Fish and shellfish cook quickly, and Essaouira fed my mind, tummy and soul with seafood. I was inspired at every turn, especially when I had dinner at Sam's – not quite the evocative Moroccan-nights' name I would have come up with for the best seafood place in town, but who am I to judge? Sam's was located at the end of the pier, past the rocking fishing boats, dried nets and slightly spooky seagulls. From the outside the restaurant looked like a blue-and-yellow lobster shack from *Family Guy*. Inside, the decor of jewel-encrusted spider crabs and black-and-white photographs of Hollywood stars was equally baffling, but the food was on the money. It was coastal Moroccan with a classic French twist – wow! All I can say is, get in a taxi right now, ask for Sam's and order the monkfish skewers. You will not be disappointed.

COCONUT, FENUGREEK AND THE BRIGHT COLOURS OF INDIA

The next stop for my research was India. Goa to be exact, where the coconut curries and fresh coastal food were all made in no time. Every town has its local food heroes, and in Dabolim it's Rita Shinde. From her beautiful garden, Rita taught the local women how to make excellent, fresh South Indian food. Now, not being local or a woman, I was very lucky she took me on. We went through all the classic Goan dishes, then she taught me about the tamarind-based Hindi food and, finally, the Catholic Goan cuisine, which used the pungent local vinegar in abundance. Her *reshado* sauce has been an utter revelation for me and I am happy to say that it has inspired several of the dishes in this book.

After Goa, I travelled north to Mumbai – a melting pot of all that India has to offer. This particular trip was made extra special by two people, Lizzie and Amish. With Lizzie's military organizational skills and Amish's local knowledge, I ate everything in Mumbai! They even arranged a low-key visit to Dharavi, one of the famed city slums. I don't know why, but for some reason I had been geared up for a massive bout of Western guilt. I expected to see horrific things, but the trip was one of the most amazing experiences I have ever had in my whole life.

The slum – wrongly named, as this suggests something bleak – is a fully functioning city within a city. Hundreds of thousands of people live, work and socialize here. Working conditions are pretty terrible, but there is life and energy like you wouldn't believe. Everyone was busy working in industry – sorting plastics, building machinery, sewing clothes, making soap and producing most of Mumbai's poppadoms. There was more of a sense of community in that place than I have ever felt before. Everyone knew each other. They chatted, they worked and they went to the high street to eat, drink, shop and even visit the cinema. The residential areas were spotless. People took pride in where they lived. For every bit of dreary grey, India's love for bright colours prevailed. For every funny odour, the wonderful smells of fenugreek and coconut oil filled the air. Even the constant noise of the traffic was drowned out by high-pitched Hindi love songs. I loved it, and even now I can feel goose bumps while I'm writing about my time there. I feel honoured to have been to Dharavi.

EATING FOR FOUR IN THE FAR EAST

The final part of my research for *Mighty Spice Express* was the Far East. Having already spent time in Thailand and Laos, I decided to freshen up my knowledge and go to Seoul and North-east China to learn something new. Seoul was bonkers – a vast metropolis of cool people, wicked food and technology that would have made the Star Trek Enterprise blush.

I kicked off my first night by exploring the low-level restaurants that lined the cross streets between the skyscrapers of Gangnam District. For some reason, every restaurant I went into threw me out. Tired and hungry, and feeling a bit like I hadn't been picked for the sports team, I retired to my hotel. Thankfully, the next day I was informed that it was not because I was weird and Western, but because the restaurants in question served huge sharing dishes that were way too big for one person. Armed with this invaluable local information I returned, asked for a table for four and ate the lot.

The next morning, my guide took me around the north of the city. First I learnt how to make precious kimchi, which is the cornerstone of every Korean meal. Next, we went on a serious street-food tour. We ate so well – *pa jun*, a fantastic Korean pancake; giant steamed dumplings filled with pork and spring onions; *bibimbap*, a classic rice dish; grilled kebabs; noodle soup with clams; and spicy fried tofu. It seemed endless – and all delicious.

AIRBORNE EXERCISES AND SPECTACULAR BARBECUES

There are not enough superlatives in the world for me to describe China. Shanghai, for example, is the only place where you can order scorpion, dim sum, sea cucumber and foie gras all at once. Several years ago my great mates, Mike and Annie, introduced me to the food of Dongbai, an area of North-east China where Annie was born. Since then, I have been obsessed with going to this part of the world, and luckily it fitted the bill for *Mighty Spice Express*. I found myself on a flight with Mike and Annie heading to the city of Shenyang to learn about Dongbai food and their famous barbecue. All that I love about China happened on that flight. At one point, the stoic passengers, who had sat so silently, were drawn to attention by the cabin crew who had formed a line down the middle of the plane. They proceeded to demonstrate a series of exercises intended to help combat cramp and deep vein thrombosis that wouldn't have looked out of place at a Spice Girls concert. The silence broke and everyone joined in expressively copying the moves. The routine culminated in hands that were crossed over shoulders, then flying into the air for an ecstatic double clap, and then the passengers returned to the demure silence of before. It was amazing and so random, just like the rest of the country.

We went straight from the airport to a restaurant called Little South Island BBQ that was owned by a friend of Annie's. It was here that I learnt the secret of Dongbai food, their barbecue and the true meaning of Chinese hospitality. Lots of things in China happen behind closed doors, including "cutting loose", which is exactly what happened at lunch. While the rest of the restaurant was filled with hushed diners, we were holed up in a private room surrounded by friends, family, food and way too much alcohol. Every sublime dish was lovingly explained to me by my hosts and followed by a lethal dose of *baiju*, a gigantically boozy Chinese liquor. We must have eaten about 40 different dishes. You can do the maths for the shots! Both the food and barbecue were an eye opener, and I learnt techniques and seasonings that I had never seen before – boy, are you in for a treat!

ABOUT THIS BOOK

Mighty Spice Express is all about fantastic food in no time. To achieve this, I have developed recipes using techniques, spices, cuts of meat and fish, cooking methods and ingredients that all work towards making delicious express meals and snacks for any occasion.

Spices are at the heart of the recipes in this book. The more I travel the more I learn new ways to use these fabulous ingredients. They are truly versatile and it's fascinating how the same spices, used in a different way, can take the food on your table from one country to another. For me, spices offer an escape and transport me somewhere else while I eat. They add the flavours, colour, heat and smell of some of the most beautiful and exotic places in the world. With a pinch of cumin, a grating of ginger or a few slices of lemongrass I can whip up something wonderful and transform my little apartment in East London into the best exotic restaurant in the world.

As you look through the book, you'll see that each recipe includes pictures of the spices used, so you'll be able to see at a glance which ones you need to make it.

This book is packed full of exciting recipes, which all work in the times I have given. I have lovingly time-tested each one, over and over again, to make sure that they all work perfectly. The key was getting the preparation and cooking done at exactly the right time. So that you can achieve the same fast results, I have included all the preparation in the recipe method rather than in the ingredients list. While part of the dish is cooking you'll be preparing the ingredients for the next stage. The recipes are not complicated, and the way I have designed them means you'll be making the most of your time in the kitchen. As long as you don't go off piste you'll nail the recipes easily.

I hope you'll enjoy making and eating this collection of recipes as much as I do and that this book will help to make cooking any meal an express experience for you.

EXPRESS FLAVOUR ESSENTIALS

Stuff your store-cupboard and stock up your fridge with some basics and you'll be able to rustle up a spicy meal at any time.

A LITTLE SOUTH-EAST ASIA

Coconut Creamed coconut is fresh coconut formed into a solid block. The high fat content means it will melt into a sauce to thicken and enrich it. It can also be grated over salads and grilled meats where it will melt through the food. Coconut cream and coconut milk are made by squeezing water through the ground flesh of a fresh coconut. The milky liquid from the first press is coconut cream. It has the highest fat content, making it rich and flavoursome. The remaining pulp is mixed with more water for a second pressing, giving the slightly milder-tasting coconut milk.

Fish sauce This smelly sauce is salty and pungent. It can be used instead of salt and to add flavour to curries, soups, stir-fries and salads.

Hoisin sauce is a Chinese condiment that can be used in stir-fries and as a dip for roasted meats, fish and vegetables. It has a rich soy–salty taste and it doesn't need cooking.

Oyster sauce is a slightly sweet condiment that is used all over South-east Asia. The thick brown sauce is made from soya beans and oyster extract, tasting both sweet and savoury. Look for the highest percentage of oyster extract when purchasing.

Rice wine vinegar This is a classic South-east Asian sour flavour. It's great for dipping sauces and salad dressings. The taste is very tart, so it always needs to be balanced by something sweet or hot.

Soy sauce The brilliant *umami* taste (meaning 'pleasant savoury taste' in Japanese) that soy sauce gives to food is superb. Use it in stews instead of salt to create depth of flavour. I have used light and dark soy sauces here. Traditionally, light is used as a seasoning and dark to add colour. I find the light salty and fresh, and the dark much richer with a more complex flavour.

Sweet chilli sauce is the ultimate ready-made dipping sauce. It works especially well in a salad dressing with a good squeeze of lime to balance out the sweetness. It's instant flavour with zero effort.

FAVE SAVOURIES

Pitted olives Olives have a good savoury taste that complements many dishes. Scatter them over salads and tagines, or use them in a salsa or pesto where their intense saltiness works really well.

Preserved lemons possess a superb and unique flavour, and are now easy to buy. Just cut them into quarters, remove and discard the flesh and finely chop or slice the skin. They work in tagines, stews, soups, salads, rice dishes and kebabs, and they provide an instant Moroccan flavour.

Sun-dried tomatoes and paste For this book I have used sun-dried tomatoes (in oil) in salsas and sauces for their intense smoky and salty flavour. The paste adds the same big flavour without chopping or blending.

Tahini Made with sesame seeds, tahini is a classic Middle Eastern ingredient. The flavour is rich and intense, and a little goes a long way. It works well as a dip mixed with yogurt and is one of the main ingredients in hummus. It lasts for ages, so you'll get lots of use from one jar.

Tomato passata and purée So many recipes are tomato-based, and if you are short of time, tomato passata and purée can be a quick solution for adding flavour. They are already cooked, so the tomato richness is intensified, and they just need to be reheated.

Worcestershire sauce This quintessentially British ingredient is bound to be lying around in one of your kitchen cupboards. It's made from vinegar, anchovies and spices, so it's not that far removed from the fishy South-east Asian condiments. It adds an unusual flavour, which melts into the background when used in curries, spice pastes and salad dressings.

VERSATILE SPICES

Chilli powder and chilli flakes Sometimes there's no time for chopping, so having chilli powder and chilli flakes to hand means an instant spicy kick.

Chinese five-spice powder is a mixture of spices, including star anise, fennel, cinnamon, cloves, Sichuan pepper, ginger and nutmeg, and there are endless combinations. It has a strong aniseed flavour that works well with soy sauce, making it perfect to add to Chinese dishes.

Chipotle chillies These are wood-smoked jalapeños, which add an incredibly woody, smoky flavour to everything – salsas, stews, spice rubs and marinades. The taste is authentically Mexican. The chillies are dried and need a little soaking in warm water or a hot sauce to soften. They also blend into a powder easily, which is perfect for salsas, rubs or marinades.

Chocolate, made from cacao, is a very old spice that was used by the Mayans of Central America. The cacao beans are roasted and mixed with cocoa butter and sugar. It has a rich, spicy and nutty flavour, which develops on your palate as it melts. Use it in sweet and savoury dishes, and buy the darkest chocolate with the highest cocoa content for cooking.

Cinnamon is a classic spice that is used the world over. It loves everything from lamb and rice to chocolate and ice cream. I use ground and sticks in my recipes, but if you don't have sticks in the cupboard, you can also substitute ½ teaspoon ground cinnamon for a 5cm/2in stick.

Cumin and coriander These are the two ingredients that I would recommend to anyone who is starting to use spices. They have a wonderful flavour, they work beautifully together and can be used in many types of cuisines. Have both ground cumin and the seeds to hand, so that you can use the seeds as a base in hot oil to flavour a dish and add some texture.

Smoked paprika The flavour-to-effort ratio of this superb spice is off the scale, which makes it my store-cupboard essential. The bright red powder is made of ground wood-smoked peppers and/or chillies, which have a massive smoky taste. You can add it to any savoury dish to inject some flavour, as well as using it in salsas, marinades, rubs and salad dressings.

THE RIGHT OIL AND VINEGAR FOR THE JOB

Groundnut oil is the best oil for making stir-fries, because it has a high smoke point, which is important when frying over a high heat. It also has a mild flavour so it won't interfere with the other flavours in the dish.

Olive oil and extra virgin olive oil have a much stronger flavour than other oils. This is great for cooking Mediterranean-style dishes and making salad dressings. Use the olive oil for cooking and the extra virgin olive oil for dressings, as it loses flavour once heated. All olive oils have a low smoke point and are not suitable for cooking over a fierce heat, such as stir-frying.

Sesame oil has a rich, roasted-sesame flavour that is perfect in salad dressings, rubs and marinades. Excellent, too, added at the end of a stir-fry.

Sunflower oil has a high smoke point. It's very mild in flavour and cheap to buy. I use it for shallow- and deep-frying in this book.

Balsamic vinegar This classic Italian sweet vinegar is great for roasts, stir-fries and salad dressings.

Cider vinegar is a versatile vinegar. It is not too tart and it works well as a substitute if you can't find rice wine vinegar.

Red wine vinegar has a lovely flavour that is not as sharp as the other vinegars and is perfect to use in cooking and as a base for salad dressings.

FRESH FLAVOURINGS

Garlic is a staple ingredient in every kitchen I have visited all over the world. It adds a sweet, mellow background flavour when cooked slowly, or a stronger fiery flavour when cooked quickly.

Ginger has a fresh peppery taste that is wonderful in curries, stir-fries and salad dressings. Fresh ginger will last in the fridge for up to a week.

Green and red chillies Fresh chillies last up to 10 days in the fridge and add heat and vibrancy to dishes both savoury and sweet. I love to have multiple chilli options at home for my cooking.

Lemongrass can make a curry taste fragrant and authentic, and the delicate citrus flavour will transform a stir-fry. It goes well with soy sauce – particularly in marinades. Stored in the fridge it will last for several weeks.

Lemons and limes All recipes need balance, and "sour" is a key flavour in South-east Asian cooking. Lemons and limes freshen everything up and ignite other flavours to make them stronger.

Parsley and coriander These two awesome herbs add colour and freshness to everything. I can't live without them. Store them in the fridge.

MIGHTY BITES

Here is a collection of my favourite snacks, and they are bursting with different flavours from around the world. Loads of the recipes were inspired by street food, which is quite simply the best fast food there is. Many are great for parties, when you want something to munch on while standing and having a chat with friends, holding a drink in your other hand. With recipes ranging from Los Danzantes Empanadas, made with prawns and mozzarella, to spicy Thai Pork Sliders, all the recipes serve 2 and there is something here for everyone. My Fried Chilli Corn, sprinkled with sea salt, is quite literally "TV sport and cold beers" best mate, but the greatest part about Mighty Bites is that all the recipes can be thrown together in 15 minutes or less.

Chicken Fillets with Sweet Chilli & Basil Sauce SERVES **2** READY IN **10 MINUTES**

I am a sucker for chicken with a dip. This is probably a hangover from my dad's obsession with chicken and mayonnaise! My cheeky chicken snack uses little chicken fillets that cook in no time. It's served with a punchy dipping sauce that is made with sweet chilli sauce, fresh green basil and wonderful fennel seeds, which liven it up with a background hint of aniseed.

4 mini chicken fillets (about
   200g/7oz total weight)
2½ tbsp olive oil
1 handful of basil leaves
1 tsp fennel seeds

3 tbsp sweet chilli sauce
½ lime
sea salt and freshly ground
   black pepper

HEAT A GRIDDLE over a high heat until smoking. Meanwhile, brush the chicken with ½ tablespoon of the oil. Lay it in the griddle and reduce the heat to medium. Griddle the chicken for 3–4 minutes on each side until golden and cooked through.

WHILE THE CHICKEN COOKS, put the basil, the remaining oil and a good pinch of salt and pepper into a mini food processor or blender, and blend until smooth. Pour the oil mixture into a serving bowl. Gently crush the fennel seeds with the back of a knife or using a mortar and pestle, and add them to the serving bowl. Add the sweet chilli sauce, then squeeze in the juice from the lime and mix well. Serve the golden chicken with the sweet chilli and basil sauce.

Blue Gate Fez Sandwich SERVES **2** READY IN **15 MINUTES**

This awesome sandwich was inspired by a street-food vendor who was parked beside the magnificent Blue Gate in Fez, Morocco. It was a freezing-cold morning, and this wicked sandwich, packed with crunchy onions, spices and fresh herbs, was the perfect way to warm up. My version uses chicken instead of offal (sorry Fez) but it shares the big flavours.

2 skinless chicken breasts
1 tbsp olive oil
½ red onion
½ lemon
8 pitted green olives
1 handful of parsley leaves
2 wholemeal bread rolls

2 tbsp sun-dried tomato paste
3 tbsp mayonnaise
½ tsp ground cumin
a pinch of chilli powder
sea salt and freshly ground
  black pepper

LAY THE CHICKEN BREASTS on a chopping board and, using a rolling pin, bash them out until they are 1cm/½in thick. Season one side with a good pinch of salt and pepper. Heat the oil in a large frying pan over a medium heat and fry the chicken, seasoned-side down, for 3–3½ minutes on each side until golden and cooked through.

WHILE THE CHICKEN COOKS, peel and slice the onion into thin strips, then put it in a mixing bowl. Squeeze over the juice from the lemon and mix well. Finely chop the olives and parsley and leave to one side.

CUT THE BREAD ROLLS IN HALF and spread the sun-dried tomato paste over one half of each roll, and the mayonnaise over the other half. Lay the cooked chicken over the base of the rolls and season with the cumin and chilli powder. Put the onions, olives and parsley over the top of the chicken, and put the other half of each roll on top. Serve immediately while hot.

Thai Pork Sliders SERVES **2**   READY IN **10 MINUTES**

These lovely little sliders (small burgers) are so tasty and quick to make. Using a really good-quality pork sausage means that the meat is already the perfect consistency to incorporate all the fragrant Thai seasonings. A fresh lime hit at the end accentuates the flavours, and the sweet chilli sauce is the perfect dunking partner.

1cm/½in piece fresh root ginger
1 garlic clove
1 lemongrass stalk
½ red chilli
¼ tsp freshly ground black pepper

1 small handful of basil leaves
1 tsp fish sauce
200g/7oz best-quality pork
  sausages
1 tbsp olive oil

TO SERVE
1 lime
sweet chilli sauce

PEEL THE GINGER and garlic, then remove the tough outer leaves from the lemongrass and cut off the ends of the stalks. Put the ginger and garlic into a mini food processor, and add the lemongrass, chilli, black pepper, basil and fish sauce. Blend into a smooth paste. Scoop the paste into a mixing bowl and leave to one side.

CUT OPEN THE SAUSAGES, peel off the skins and chuck the meat into the mixing bowl with the spice paste. Mix everything together well and divide the pork into 6 portions. Flatten each portion into the shape of a mini burger – *voila* sliders!

HEAT THE OIL in a large frying pan over a medium heat and fry the sliders for 1½–2 minutes on each side until golden and crispy.

WHILE THE PORK COOKS, cut the lime in half and pour the sweet chilli sauce into a serving bowl. Serve the sliders with the lime and sweet chilli sauce.

Hummus Beiruti SERVES **2** READY IN **10 MINUTES**

To me, hummus rocks! My Hummus Beiruti is a slightly tarted-up version of the awesome dip. I make a deliciously light hummus, then top it with lovely sweet lamb that has been fried, super-fast, with allspice, cumin and cinnamon. The hit of spiced lamb melts through the hummus and makes it even more unbelievably tasty. This is ready in less than 10 minutes, so there's always time for a bit of happy hummus eating.

4 tbsp olive oil
115g/4oz minced lamb
¼ tsp ground allspice
¼ tsp ground cumin
a pinch of ground cinnamon

1½ lemons
2 pitta breads
400g/14oz/scant 2 cups tinned
   chickpeas
1 garlic clove

2 tbsp tahini
sea salt

HEAT 1 TABLESPOON OF THE OIL in a frying pan over a high heat and add the lamb. Stir-fry for 2 minutes, then reduce the heat to medium. Add the allspice, cumin and cinnamon, and squeeze in the juice of ½ lemon. Cook for 2–3 minutes, stirring occasionally, until the lamb is cooked through.

WHILE THE LAMB COOKS, pop the pitta breads into a toaster and toast until crunchy. Chuck the chickpeas in a colander and give them a good rinse. Drain off any excess water and put them into a blender or food processor with the remaining olive oil. Peel the garlic and add it to the blender with the tahini and 55ml/1¾fl oz/ scant ¼ cup water. Season with salt. Squeeze in the juice of the remaining lemon and blend until smooth. Serve the hummus topped with the lamb and with the toasted pitta for dunking.

Korean Kebabs SERVES 2   READY IN **10 MINUTES**

As I roamed the high-tech streets of Seoul in Korea, I found little food stalls nestled in the side streets offering the tastiest snacks. My favourites were these beef kebabs, which were barbecued over hot coals and served with a brushing of sticky marinade and crunchy sesame seeds. What is great about them is that they are so quick and easy to make yet they taste out of this world.

175g/6oz fillet steak
1 garlic clove
1½ tbsp soy sauce
2 tsp clear honey

½ tsp freshly ground black pepper
1 tsp sesame oil
½ tsp groundnut oil
1 tsp sesame seeds

CUT THE STEAK into long, thin strips, about 2mm/1⁄16in thick, and put them in a mixing bowl.

HEAT A GRIDDLE over a high heat until smoking. Meanwhile, peel and crush the garlic into the bowl with the steak, and add the soy sauce, honey, black pepper, sesame oil and groundnut oil. Mix well to coat, then thread the strips of steak on to six metal skewers.

GRIDDLE THE KEBABS for 1–1½ minutes on each side until charred but still pink and juicy in the centre. Transfer the kebabs to a serving dish, scatter over the sesame seeds and serve.

Moroccan Paper Bag Sardines SERVES **2** READY IN **15 MINUTES**

I first ate this fabulous snack in Fez. After a hard day's eating, I stopped at a tiny hole-in-the-wall where I was served crispy sardines in a paper bag with a wedge of lemon. What I loved was the texture of the batter. It was an even mix of flour and semolina, which gave even more crunch to the fish. The subtle spicing, which was mixed into the batter, really brought it to life. Just a little cumin and chilli powder, and you're away.

sunflower oil, for shallow-frying
50g/1¾oz/heaped ⅓ cup plain
　flour
50g/1¾oz/heaped ⅓ cup semolina
2 tsp ground cumin
1 tsp chilli powder

8 small sardines, cleaned
150g/5½oz/scant ⅔ cup yogurt
1 tsp harissa or chilli paste
1 lemon
sea salt

POUR THE OIL into a large frying pan to a depth of 1cm/½in and heat over a medium-high heat. Meanwhile, sift the flour into a large mixing bowl and add the semolina, cumin and chilli powder, then season with salt. Pour in 150ml/5fl oz/scant ⅔ cup cold water and whisk into a thick batter. Add the sardines and gently mix to coat them completely in the batter.

SHAKE ANY EXCESS BATTER off the sardines and shallow-fry them in the hot oil for 3–4 minutes on each side until beautifully golden and cooked through. Carefully remove the sardines from the oil and put them on to kitchen paper to drain.

WHILE THE SARDINES DRAIN, tip the yogurt into a serving bowl and add the harissa. Lightly season with salt and mix well. Cut the lemon into wedges. Serve the sardines with the harissa yogurt and lemon wedges.

Crab & Spring Onion Pancakes SERVES 2 READY IN **15 MINUTES**

This is a classic Korean snack and one that I know you'll love. It's actually called *pa-jun* and is an eggy pancake flavoured with soy and chilli, then stuffed with beautifully sweet crab meat, fresh herbs and oyster sauce. Typically, it would be served with a spicy *kimchi* – if you can get hold of some, give it a whirl. But it really is just so good on its own.

40g/1½oz/⅓ cup plain flour
1 egg
¼ tsp crushed chilli flakes
1 tsp light soy sauce
3 spring onions
1 handful of coriander leaves

100g/3½oz/scant ⅔ cup cooked
  white crab meat
1cm/½in piece fresh root ginger
1 tbsp groundnut oil
2 tbsp oyster sauce

TIP THE FLOUR into a large mixing bowl, pour in 60ml/2fl oz/¼ cup water and crack in the egg. Season with the chilli flakes and soy sauce, and whisk everything together into a smooth batter.

TRIM THE SPRING ONIONS, then finely chop the spring onions and coriander, and put half in the batter. Mix well. Put the other half into a separate mixing bowl and add the crab. Peel the ginger, then grate it over the crab and mix well.

HEAT HALF THE OIL in a large frying pan over a medium heat and pour in half the batter mix. Cook for 1 minute on each side, then transfer to a serving plate. Keep the pancake warm while you cook a second pancake in the same way.

BRUSH THE TOP OF EACH PANCAKE with a quarter of the oyster sauce. Divide the crab mixture into 2 portions and arrange 1 portion in a line down the centre of each pancake. Fold the pancakes in half and transfer them to serving plates. Drizzle the remaining oyster sauce over each portion and serve.

Jonny's Dumplings SERVES 2 READY IN **15 MINUTES**

Dim sum is somewhat of an obsession of mine. From the super-slimy rice rolls to the dry, delicate, steamed parcels of a high-brow Hong Kong hotel, I can't get enough. The ritual of ticking the little boxes on the menu, waiting for the steamer trolley and then dipping the glory into various soy, chilli and vinegar condiments is a complete pleasure to me. To make, though, it's not so fun. However, I really wanted to get something into this book, and after eating cabbage-leaf dim sum at a restaurant called Jonny's in Korea, I thought, "bring it on", and I came up with this quick version.

2 large green savoy cabbage leaves
¼ red chilli
1 spring onion
1 small handful of coriander leaves

150g/5½oz raw, peeled king
  prawns
¼ tsp Chinese five-spice powder

1 tsp light soy sauce, plus extra
  to serve
1 tbsp groundnut oil

PUT THE CABBAGE LEAVES in a heatproof bowl and cover with boiling water. Leave to soften for 2–3 minutes. Meanwhile, deseed the chilli and trim the spring onion. Chuck them both into a blender or food processor and add the coriander, prawns, Chinese five-spice powder and soy sauce. Blend until smooth.

DRAIN THE CABBAGE LEAVES in a colander and refresh under cold water for a few seconds until they are cool enough to handle. Gently squeeze out any excess water and put on to a chopping board. Cut out the stems and cut the leaves into 2 halves. Put a quarter of the prawn mixture on to each piece of cabbage leaf and roll them up, tucking in the sides. They should look like roundish spring rolls.

HEAT THE OIL in a frying pan over a high heat and add the dumplings, fold-side down. Cook for 2 minutes, then pour boiling water into the side of the frying pan to a depth of 2mm/¹⁄₁₆in. Cover, reduce the heat to medium and steam for 4 minutes. Remove the lid and cook for 2–3 minutes until most of the water has evaporated and the dumplings are cooked through. Serve with light soy sauce for dipping.

Los Danzantes Empanadas SERVES **2** READY IN **10 MINUTES**

Traditionally, *empanadas* are deep-fried Mexican snacks that look like little Cornish pasties. They are crunchy and delicious, but quite time-consuming to make. These *empanadas* are an express version. I use a soft flour tortilla for the shell, stuff it with prawns, mozzarella, smoky sun-dried tomatoes, chilli, spring onions and coriander, then pan-fry it to get a crispy outside and an oozing filling. As they take only 10 minutes to make, I am sure you'll forgive me for not being an *empanada* purist.

2 spring onions
¼ red chilli
55g/2oz/heaped ⅓ cup drained
  sun-dried tomatoes in oil
1 small handful of coriander leaves

1 flour tortilla
1 tbsp olive oil
60g/2¼oz mozzarella cheese
100g/3½oz cooked, peeled prawns
¼ lime

TRIM THE SPRING ONIONS, then chuck them into a mini food processor, and add the chilli, sun-dried tomatoes and coriander, and blend into a rough paste. Lay the tortilla on a chopping board and spread the paste over the top, leaving a 1cm/½in gap around the edge.

HEAT THE OIL in a non-stick frying pan over a high heat. Meanwhile, tear the mozzarella into bite-sized pieces and put it, with the prawns, over one half of the tortilla. Wet your finger under the cold tap and then rub it around the border of the tortilla. Fold the tortilla in half and press the edges together to keep it sealed.

CAREFULLY PUT THE EMPANADA in the hot pan, reduce the heat to medium and cook for 1½–2 minutes on each side until warmed through and golden. Cut the empanada in half and transfer to serving plates. Cut the lime quarter in half and serve with each empanada.

Dosa Rosti SERVES **2** READY IN **15 MINUTES**

My *dosa rosti* is a super-quick South Indian-inspired snack. The grated potato and onion cook down fast and take on all the flavour of the spices. I love the added layer of heat from the hot lime pickle slathered over the roti. This is fast food, Indian-style.

1 large potato (about 200g/7oz)	1 tsp mustard seeds
½ red onion	1 tomato
1 tsp ground cumin	1 handful of coriander leaves
1 tsp ground coriander	2 plain roti
¼ tsp chilli powder	1 tbsp hot lime pickle
¼ tsp turmeric	½ lime
2 tbsp groundnut oil	sea salt

PEEL THE POTATO and onion, then grate both into a mixing bowl. Add the cumin, coriander, chilli powder and turmeric, and season with salt, then mix everything together well.

HEAT THE OIL in a large frying pan over a high heat and add the mustard seeds. Allow them to crackle for a couple of seconds, then tip in the potatoes and onion, and stir-fry for 3 minutes. Add 100ml/3½fl oz/generous ⅓ cup water, mix well, then cover and reduce the heat to medium. Cook for 4–5 minutes, stirring occasionally, until soft.

WHILE THE POTATO COOKS, cut the tomato in half, squeeze out the seeds and finely chop the flesh. Finely chop the coriander leaves and leave to one side.

PUT THE ROTI on to a chopping board and spread the lime pickle evenly over each one. To serve the dish, squeeze the juice from the lime into the cooked potatoes and mix well. Divide the potato mixture between each roti, scatter over the tomato and coriander leaves, and serve.

MUMBAI MAGIC, HOLY COWS & PANEER

The city of Mumbai thrives on street food. It feeds the masses. If you are looking for a quick lunch, a tasty snack or a refreshing drink, Mumbai has it all. The people are fiercely loyal to their favourite vendors, some of which have been around for generations. In fact, my friends Lizzie and Amish had a *chai*-off, both taking me to their favourite *chai wallahs* and tutting at the thought of me drinking and enjoying the other's brew – just for the record, guys, I enjoyed the Indian Stock Exchange *chai* the most!

I sped through the city on the back of my friend's motorbike, weaving between the blacked-out Mercs, rickshaws, carts and sleeping cows to get to the finest street-food vendors. We ate *chaats* and *pakoras* at Chhatrapati Shivaji terminus, and Parsi sweets on Marine Drive, we sampled the various *puris* and *kulfi* from Chowpatty Beach and drank salted *lassis* from clay mugs in the backstreets of Dharavi.

One smoky stall grilled up chunks of paneer and doused them in a super-spicy green chutney. It was fantastic. The slightly chewy, bland paneer was the perfect vehicle for the explosive chutney – absorbing all the flavour and some of the heat. The dish was simple to prepare, overwhelmingly tasty and took just minutes to make.

Griddled Paneer with Mint Chutney SERVES **2** READY IN **10 MINUTES**

For my version of the classic Indian snack, grilled paneer, I have added a little coconut to the chutney, as it works so well with the mint, chilli and ground coriander. It also seems to bring all those fresh ingredients together so that their flavours combine into something new. Mr Paneer Wallah on Uah Kham Murg in sunny Mumbai – I hope I have done you proud.

1 green chilli
¼ red onion
2 large handfuls of mint leaves
½ tsp ground coriander
1 tomato

30g/1oz creamed coconut
½ lemon
150g/5½oz paneer
1 tbsp olive oil
sea salt

CUT THE TOP OFF THE CHILLI and roll the chilli between your hands to deseed it, then put it into a mini food processor. Peel the onion and add it to the food processor. Strip in the mint leaves, then add the coriander, tomato, coconut and 3 tablespoons water, and season with salt. Squeeze in the juice from the lemon. Blend until smooth and pour into a serving bowl. Cover and leave to one side.

HEAT A GRIDDLE over a high heat until smoking. Meanwhile, cut the paneer into pieces 1cm/½in thick and brush each piece with a little oil. Griddle for 1–1½ minutes on each side until charred with perfect griddle lines. Transfer to a serving plate and serve with the madly green mint chutney.

Fried Chilli Corn SERVES **2** READY IN **10 MINUTES**

A few years ago I was in Thailand for New Year's Eve with all the family. We stayed in a beautiful house on Phuket where we were completely spoiled by the fantastic chef, Jitty. Jitty could cook like an angel sent from cooking heaven, and every meal was a complete pleasure to eat. She realized that she had a bunch of very greedy Brits, which opened up the floodgates to snacks throughout the day. Her awesome corn was served as the sun went down, with an ice-cold beer by the pool. I can't give you Thai sunsets or a pool, but make this corn, grab a beer and you'll be just as happy.

750ml/26fl oz/3 cups sunflower oil
250g/9oz/1⅔ cups tinned
   sweetcorn
4 tbsp cornflour

1 tsp chilli powder
1 tsp Chinese five-spice powder
sea salt

HEAT THE OIL in a deep pan over a high heat. Meanwhile, drain the sweetcorn thoroughly in a colander. Tip it into a mixing bowl and add the cornflour, chilli powder, Chinese five-spice powder and 1½ tablespoons cold water. Mix everything together well so that the sweetcorn is completely coated with the cornflour and spices.

USING A SLOTTED SPOON, carefully transfer the corn to the hot oil. Stir, then deep-fry for 3 minutes, or until golden and crunchy. Remove from the oil and drain very well on kitchen paper. Tip the sweetcorn into serving bowls and season with salt. Serve with ice-cold beers.

NOT QUITE LUNCH

Here are my favourite recipes for a lazy breakfast, early lunch or brunch. They remind me of being on holiday, which is only ever a good thing – when you can get up at your own pace and eat a long, leisurely meal in the early morning. My Baked Eggs with Lentils & Goat's Cheese take only 15 minutes to make and are a winner every time. Fantastic Cochin Crab Cakes, flavoured with curry leaves and chilli, will transport you to the hot, breezy shores of South India. And my beautifully sweet Villa Dinari Apricots, swollen in orange juice, cinnamon and honey, and served warm with yogurt, can be put together in just 10 minutes. The most a recipe in this chapter will take to prepare and cook is 25 minutes.

Chorizo & Chilli Focaccia SERVES **2**   READY IN **10 MINUTES**

This super-fast dish is basically an open sandwich. The chorizo filling does most of the work and the fennel seeds, chilli and garlic make it taste even better. Juicy cherry tomatoes, peppery rocket and salty pecorino add all the extra flavours you need to make one heck of a sandwich – and it only takes 10 minutes to prepare and cook.

200g/7oz focaccia
1½ tbsp olive oil, plus extra to serve
150g/5½oz chorizo, in one piece
2 garlic cloves

1 tsp fennel seeds
¼ tsp crushed chilli flakes
100g/3½oz/heaped ⅔ cup cherry tomatoes
1 lemon

2 handfuls of rocket
30g/1oz pecorino cheese

PREHEAT THE GRILL to high. Meanwhile, cut the focaccia in half horizontally and carefully scoop out a little of the centre from each half using your fingers. Drizzle ½ tablespoon of the oil over both halves and grill for 2½–3 minutes until golden.

WHILE THE FOCACCIA COOKS, slice the chorizo into bite-sized pieces. Peel and slice the garlic into slithers. Heat the remaining oil in a frying pan over a medium heat and add the chorizo, garlic, fennel seeds and chilli flakes. Mix everything together well and cook for 3–4 minutes, stirring occasionally, until the chorizo starts turning golden at the edges.

CUT THE CHERRY TOMATOES into quarters while the chorizo cooks, then put them into the centres of the grilled focaccia halves.

PUT THE FOCACCIA on to a chopping board. Cut the lemon in half and squeeze the juice from 1 half into the pan with the chorizo, then mix well. Tip the delicious golden chorizo on to the focaccia, along with all the juices from the pan. Scatter over the rocket and shave over the cheese. Serve with the remaining lemon and a bottle of olive oil at the table.

MIGHTY MOSQUES, BRIGHT BLUE BOSPORUS & TURKISH PIZZAS

Istanbul is such a stunning city. It spans both sides of the mighty Bosporus, a strait that marks the divide between Europe and Asia. The Europe side is home to the beautiful Blue Mosque, whose huge minarets dwarf the surrounding buildings, and the amazing Grand Bazaar, which is filled with spices, dried fruits and snacks. A quick boat trip across the sparkling turquoise waters takes you to the Asia side of the city, which has a much more laid-back feel than the majestic Europe side.

When I took the boat across the river to the Asia side of the city it was match day between Istanbul Buyuk and Ankaraspor. I am pleased to say that Istanbul thrashed them 3–0! Match day meant that food was everywhere. It was awesome. We wandered around soaking up the atmosphere, sipping ice-cold beers and munching on delicious snacks, such as *kasarli*, a Turkish cheese sandwich, and yummy *simit*, a chewy ring of bread covered in crunchy sesame seeds, as well as tangy fish and onion kebabs.

All the street food was accompanied by little glass shakers filled with blood-red Turkish chilli flakes. The chilli flakes have a mild, smoky flavour, like a mix of a sun-dried tomato and dried red chilli. The rich flavour worked beautifully with all the charcoal-grilled food.

The street food that did it for me the most was *lahmacun*, or Turkish pizza. This fabulous snack, which could thankfully be found all over the city, had a crispy, chewy base that was covered in minced beef or lamb, spices, tomato and herbs. It was always served with those wonderful chilli flakes and with wedges of lemon to freshen it up and exaggerate all those flavours. I fell in love with this snack and am pleased to say that I have made a super-fast version – my Lahmacun Turkish Pizza can be made in just 10 minutes.

Lahmacun – Turkish Pizza SERVES **2** READY IN **10 MINUTES**

1½ tbsp olive oil
200g/7oz minced lamb
2 garlic cloves
½ tsp sweet paprika
½ tsp ground cumin
¼ tsp ground cinnamon
1 lemon

½ tomato
1 tbsp sun-dried tomato paste
2 flour tortillas
1 small handful of mint leaves
1 small handful of parsley leaves
a pinch of crushed chilli flakes
sea salt

PREHEAT THE GRILL to high. Meanwhile, heat 1 tablespoon of the oil in a large frying pan over a high heat. Add the lamb and stir well. Peel and crush over the garlic, and add the paprika, cumin and cinnamon, then season with salt. Squeeze over the juice of ½ lemon and stir-fry for 3–4 minutes until the lamb is cooked through and golden. Remove from the heat and leave to one side.

SQUEEZE OUT THE SEEDS from the tomato half, then finely chop the flesh. Chuck the tomato into the cooked lamb and add the sun-dried tomato paste. Mix well.

PUT THE TORTILLAS on to a grill rack and brush with the remaining oil. Spoon over the spicy lamb and grill for 1–2 minutes until the tortillas start to crisp up at the edges.

WHILE THE LAHMACUN COOKS, finely chop the herbs and cut the remaining lemon half into quarters. Scatter the herbs and chilli flakes over the cooked lahmacun and serve with the lemon wedges.

Scrambled Eggs with Lime & Ginger Smoked Salmon SERVES **2**   READY IN **10 MINUTES**

Smoked salmon is a great express ingredient. It's bursting with flavour and you don't have to do anything to it. I have simply jazzed up the salmon with a lovely oriental dressing made from soy sauce, sesame oil, chilli powder, lime juice and ginger, all of which complement the oily fish. The addition of a bagel and some creamy eggs takes it into a breakfast place, and the pumpkin seeds add some texture.

1½ tsp soy sauce
½ tsp sesame oil
a pinch of chilli powder
1 lime
5mm/¼in piece fresh root ginger

140g/5oz sliced smoked salmon
1 bagel
10g/¼oz butter
4 eggs
6 chives

1 handful of baby spinach leaves
1 tbsp pumpkin seeds
sea salt and freshly ground black
   pepper

POUR THE SOY SAUCE and sesame oil into a shallow dish. Add the chilli powder, squeeze in the juice from the lime, then peel the ginger and grate it into the dish. Mix with a fork, then add the salmon and gently mix again. Cover and leave to one side.

CUT THE BAGEL IN HALF and put it in the toaster to toast. Meanwhile, melt the butter in a frying pan over a medium heat. Crack the eggs into a mixing bowl, season with salt and pepper and whisk well. Pour the eggs into the frying pan with the melted butter and leave for 45 seconds so that they begin to set. Stir well, then cook for another 1–2 minutes, stirring frequently, until they are 80 per cent set, then remove the pan from the heat – the eggs will continue to cook a little.

PUT EACH TOASTED BAGEL HALF on to a serving plate. Spoon over the eggs and use scissors to snip the chives over the top. Chuck the spinach and pumpkin seeds into the dish with the salmon and toss together. Divide the salmon and spinach between the two plates and serve.

Smoked Haddock & Chumula Kedgeree SERVES **2**   READY IN **20 MINUTES**

FOR THE KEDGEREE
200g/7oz/1 cup basmati rice
2 eggs
1 tbsp olive oil
140g/5oz undyed smoked haddock
85g/3oz/½ cup frozen peas
3 cardamom pods

2 tbsp double cream (optional)
freshly ground black pepper

FOR THE CHUMULA
1 garlic clove
½ green chilli
2 handfuls of coriander leaves

1 handful of parsley leaves
1 tsp paprika
1 tsp ground cumin
2 tsp sugar
60ml/2fl oz/¼ cup olive oil
1 lemon
sea salt

COOK THE RICE in boiling water for 10–12 minutes until soft, or as directed on the packet. Drain in a colander and leave to one side.

WHILE THE RICE COOKS, boil the eggs in a saucepan of boiling water for 7½ minutes until perfectly medium-soft. Remove with a slotted spoon and put them in a bowl of cold water to cool.

MEANWHILE, PEEL THE GARLIC for the chumula, then chuck all the ingredients for the chumula, except the lemon, into a mini food processor or blender. Squeeze in the juice from the lemon, then season with salt. Blend into a coarse paste and leave to one side for the flavours to develop.

HEAT THE OIL for the kedgeree in a large frying pan over a low heat. Flake in the smoked haddock and add the peas and cardamom pods. Cook gently for 3–4 minutes, stirring occasionally, until the fish is cooked and the peas have warmed through. Tip in the chumula, the cooked rice and cream, if using, and season with black pepper. Carefully mix everything together and continue to cook for another 2–3 minutes for all the flavours to come together.

PEEL THE EGGS and cut them in half while the kedgeree cooks. Serve the kedgeree with the eggs.

Cochin Crab Cakes SERVES **2** READY IN **15 MINUTES**

My Cochin Crab Cakes make the perfect light meal. They are packed with juicy crab, and with tomatoes, coriander and spring onions to freshen things up. Finally, mustard seeds, curry leaves, turmeric and chilli add the flavours of South India. The hit of lime at the end accentuates all the spices even more, so in only 15 minutes you get something amazing.

2 tbsp groundnut oil
1 tsp mustard seeds
a large pinch of dried curry leaves
¼ tsp turmeric
½ tsp chilli powder
3 spring onions
5 cherry tomatoes
1 handful of coriander leaves

200g/7oz/1½ cups cooked white
  crab meat
60g/2¼oz/¾ cup fresh
  breadcrumbs
1 small egg
1 lime
sea salt

HEAT 1 TABLESPOON OF THE OIL in a small frying pan over a medium heat and add the mustard seeds. Fry for 30 seconds, shaking the pan continuously, or until the mustard seeds start popping. Rub the curry leaves between your hands so that they break into the pan, then remove the pan from the heat. Add the turmeric and chilli powder, and leave to one side.

TRIM THE SPRING ONIONS, then finely chop them with the cherry tomatoes and coriander, and chuck them all into a mixing bowl. Tip in the crab and breadcrumbs, and season with salt. Add the cooked spices and oil from the frying pan, then crack in the egg and mix everything together well. Divide the mixture into 4 and flatten each one into a crab cake about 1cm/½in thick.

HEAT THE REMAINING OIL in a large frying pan over a medium heat and fry the crab cakes for 2 minutes on each side, or until beautifully golden and warmed through. Cut the lime into wedges and serve with the hot crab cakes.

Prawn Tortas with Salsa Mexicana SERVES **2** READY IN **20 MINUTES**

FOR THE PRAWN TORTAS
200g/7oz potatoes
1 garlic clove
4 spring onions
1 handful of coriander leaves
175g/6oz raw, peeled king prawns
30g/1oz feta cheese

½ egg
80g/2¾oz/scant ⅔ cup plain flour
1 tbsp olive oil, plus extra for
   greasing
sea salt and freshly ground black
   pepper

FOR THE SALSA MEXICANA
1 garlic clove
100g/3½oz/⅔ cup drained
   sun-dried tomatoes in oil
1 dried chipotle chilli
1 tbsp olive oil
½ lime

CHOP THE UNPEELED POTATOES into 1cm/½in cubes and cook them in a saucepan of boiling water for 8 minutes, or until tender. Drain in a colander and refresh under cold water, then drain again. Return the potatoes to the saucepan and lightly mash them so that they start to break down. Leave to one side.

WHILE THE POTATOES COOK, peel the garlic and trim the spring onions, then put them into a food processor with the coriander and blend to roughly chop. Add the prawns and feta cheese, and blend into a rough paste. Tip the paste into a large mixing bowl, add the egg and flour, then season with salt and pepper. Transfer the mashed potatoes to the bowl and mix everything together well until a dough-like consistency.

HEAT THE OIL in a small frying pan over a high heat. Scoop the potato mixture into the pan and spread it out to cover the base. Reduce the heat to medium and cook for 1½–2 minutes, shaking the pan occasionally, until golden on one side.

MEANWHILE, TO MAKE THE SALSA, peel the garlic, then put it into a mini food processor or blender with the sun-dried tomatoes, chilli and oil. Squeeze in the juice from the lime, season with salt and blend into a smooth paste. Tip the smoky salsa into a serving bowl and leave to one side.

WHEN THE TORTAS HAS COOKED on one side, rub a little oil over a side plate and carefully place it, oil-side down, over the pan with the half-cooked tortas. Holding the plate and the frying pan handle, carefully flip the pan over so that the tortas rests on the plate. Slip it back into the pan and cook for another 1½–2 minutes until golden. Serve with the hot, smoky salsa.

Baked Eggs with Lentils & Goat's Cheese SERVES **2** READY IN **15 MINUTES**

At the moment, baked eggs are very trendy, and for good reason – they are delicious and require little effort. My baked eggs sit on a base of lentils, sage, chilli and spring onions. I have added sun-dried tomato paste and paprika to introduce even more flavour without taking up any extra time. A final crumble of salty goat's cheese, which melts into the eggs while they finish cooking, tops everything off perfectly.

1 garlic clove
3 spring onions
½ red chilli
8 sage leaves
2 tbsp olive oil

400g/14oz/1½ cups tinned green lentils
150g/5½oz/scant ⅔ cup tomato passata
1 tbsp sun-dried tomato paste

2 eggs
55g/2oz goat's cheese
¼ tsp paprika
2 slices of fantastic bread
sea salt and freshly ground black pepper

PREHEAT THE GRILL to high. Meanwhile, peel the garlic and trim the spring onions, then finely chop the garlic, spring onions, chilli and sage. Heat 1 tablespoon of the oil in a large ovenproof frying pan over a medium heat and add the chopped ingredients. Cook for 3–4 minutes, stirring occasionally, until the spring onions have started to soften.

DRAIN AND RINSE THE LENTILS, then tip them into the pan. Add the passata and sun-dried tomato paste, then season with a good pinch of salt and pepper. Mix everything together really well.

MAKE TWO SHALLOW WELLS in the lentil mixture and crack in the eggs. Crumble the goat's cheese over the top and put a small pinch of paprika and salt on to each egg. Grill for 4–5 minutes until the eggs have just set with a runny yolk.

POP THE BREAD INTO THE TOASTER to toast while the eggs cook. Drizzle the remaining oil over the cooked eggs and serve with the toast.

Parsi Eggs SERVES **2** READY IN **15 MINUTES**

This was my breakfast in a little Parsi café in Mumbai after a long overnight train journey from Goa. The eggs were Indianed up with loads of spices and mixed with vegetables and fresh coriander. It was the perfect start to the day in that magnificent city.

4 eggs
¼ tsp chilli powder
½ tsp ground coriander
¼ tsp garam masala
1 garlic clove
3 spring onions
1 tomato

1 handful of coriander leaves
2 slices of brown bread
1 tbsp olive oil
55g/2oz/heaped ⅓ cup frozen peas
85g/3oz/heaped ⅓ cup tinned
  sweetcorn
sea salt

CRACK THE EGGS into a mixing bowl and add the chilli powder, ground coriander and garam masala. Season with a good pinch of salt and whisk together. Leave to one side.

PEEL THE GARLIC and trim the spring onions, then finely chop the garlic, spring onions, tomato and coriander leaves. Leave to one side with the coriander in a separate pile. Put the bread in the toaster to toast while you cook the eggs.

HEAT THE OIL in a large frying pan over a high heat. Add the garlic, spring onions and tomato, then stir-fry for 2 minutes, or until the tomato starts to break down and become a little dry.

TIP IN THE PEAS and sweetcorn, then mix well. Reduce the heat to medium and pour in the eggs. Mix everything together really well and leave to set for 1 minute. Throw in the coriander and cook for 1–2 minutes, stirring continuously, until set. Serve with the toast.

Blue Mosque Goat's Cheese Tart SERVES **2** READY IN **25 MINUTES**

My goat's cheese tart is a twist on the classic Turkish snack *borek*. I have made one large tart instead of fiddly individual portions, and stuffed it with chilli, spring onions, olives, walnuts, tarragon, goat's cheese and paprika.

1 green chilli
3 spring onions
55g/2oz/scant ⅓ cup pitted green olives
55g/2oz/scant ½ cup walnuts

1 large handful of tarragon leaves
125g/4½oz soft goat's cheese
¼ tsp paprika
1 lemon
2 tbsp olive oil

3 sheets of filo pastry, defrosted if frozen
100g/3½oz/heaped ⅓ cup yogurt
sea salt and freshly ground black pepper

PREHEAT THE OVEN to 180°C/350°F/Gas 4. Cut the top off the chilli and roll the chilli between your hands to deseed it. Trim the spring onions. Put the chilli and spring onions into a food processor, and add the olives, walnuts and tarragon. Blend until coarsely chopped, then add the goat's cheese and paprika. Squeeze in the juice of ½ lemon and season with salt and pepper. Give it a quick blast to mix it all together.

TAKE A PIECE OF BAKING PARCHMENT, large enough to fit in a baking tray, and scrunch it between your hands – this stops the sides from curling up. Flatten the baking parchment on to a chopping board and brush with olive oil. Lay a piece of the filo pastry on top of the baking parchment and brush it all over with oil (cover the unused filo with a damp tea towel to prevent it from drying out). Put another piece of filo pastry over the top and brush it with oil.

SCOOP THE FILLING into the centre of the pastry and spread it out into a rectangular shape about 1.5cm/⅝in thick. Cover with the final sheet of filo pastry and fold in the sides to form a neat rectangle. Brush the top of the tart with oil and season with salt and pepper.

TRANSFER THE TART to the baking tray, by lifting up the sides of the baking parchment, then bake for 15–18 minutes until golden on top. Meanwhile, put the yogurt into a serving bowl, squeeze in the juice from the remaining ½ lemon and season with salt and pepper. Mix well. Serve the hot tart with the lemony yogurt.

Zaatar Halloumi with Couscous Salad SERVES **2** READY IN **15 MINUTES**

FOR THE ZAATAR HALLOUMI
1 tbsp sumac
1 tbsp dried oregano
3 tsp sesame seeds
200g/7oz halloumi
2 tbsp olive oil

FOR THE COUSCOUS
60g/2¼oz/⅓ cup couscous
1 red chilli
1 handful of parsley leaves
1 tbsp capers
1 tbsp olive oil

½ lemon
sea salt and freshly ground
  black pepper

TO MAKE THE ZAATAR, mix the sumac, oregano, sesame seeds and a good pinch of salt in a bowl.

PUT HALF THE ZAATAR in a large mixing bowl and tip in the couscous. Mix with a fork. Pour over 90ml/3fl oz/generous ⅓ cup warm water, cover with cling film and leave to one side to absorb the water. This will take about 10 minutes.

MEANWHILE, CUT THE TOP off the chilli and roll the chilli between your hands to deseed it, then finely chop the chilli and parsley. Drain and finely chop the capers. Leave to one side.

CUT THE HALLOUMI into 5mm/¼in slices and press each piece into the zaatar spices to cover with a thin layer on one side. Heat the oil in large frying pan over a medium heat. Add the halloumi, spice-side down, and fry for 2–3 minutes on each side until golden. Remove the pan from the heat and leave to one side while you finish the salad.

WHEN THE COUSCOUS has absorbed all the water, fluff it up with a fork, then add the olive oil and squeeze in the juice from the lemon. Chuck in the chopped chilli, parsley and capers, and add a pinch of salt, if needed, and pepper. Serve the couscous with the delicious fried halloumi.

Orange & Cardamom French Toast SERVES **2** READY IN **15 MINUTES**

For those with a sweet tooth, my Orange & Cardamom French Toast won't disappoint. The toast is cooked until crispy in a mixture of butter, cardamom, sultanas and orange. The cardamom flavours everything, and the sultanas swell up in the perfumed juices. I use maple syrup as the crowning glory, because I love the slightly smoky sweetness it gives to the overall flavour of the dish.

2 eggs
100ml/3½fl oz/generous ⅓ cup
  milk
1 orange
1 tbsp icing sugar
4 thick slices of white bread
  (about 1cm/½in thick)

40g/1½oz butter
55g/2oz/scant ½ cup sultanas
6 cardamom pods
3 tbsp maple syrup

CRACK THE EGGS into a mixing bowl and pour in the milk. Zest the orange into the bowl, add the icing sugar and whisk together. Put the bread in a shallow dish and pour over the egg mixture. Ensure that both sides of each slice of bread are well soaked so that nearly all the liquid is absorbed. Leave to one side.

PUT THE BUTTER and sultanas into a large frying pan over a medium heat. Gently crush the cardamom pods by pressing down with the side of a knife, then add them to the butter. Cut the orange into quarters and squeeze a quarter into the frying pan. Mix well and cook gently for 1 minute, or until the butter melts.

ADD THE BREAD to the pan and fry for 2½–3 minutes on each side until beautifully golden, shaking the pan occasionally. Divide between two serving plates and squeeze the remaining orange over each toast. Drizzle with the maple syrup and serve with the yummy sultanas.

Villa Dinari Apricots with Yogurt SERVES **2** READY IN **10 MINUTES**

During my time in Morocco I cooked dinner with the chefs at the beautiful Villa Dinari. We made a feast that included a particularly wonderful lamb and pear tagine, which was finished off with dried apricots that had been cooked slowly in sugar and cinnamon. They were fantastic. I thought that the apricots, with a little twist, would be excellent with a big fat bowl of creamy yogurt. For my fast breakfast version I cook the apricots for a couple of minutes in butter, orange, cinnamon and honey. Once they have swollen to capacity they go straight into bowls to be topped with some yogurt and a sprinkling of crunchy walnuts.

30g/1oz butter
150g/5½oz/generous ¾ cup ready-
  to-eat dried apricots
½ tsp ground cinnamon

2 tbsp clear honey
½ orange
250g/9oz/1 cup yogurt
55g/2oz/scant ½ cup walnuts

HEAT THE BUTTER in a frying pan over a medium heat and add the apricots, cinnamon and honey.

SQUEEZE IN THE JUICE from the orange and mix well. Cook for 5–6 minutes, stirring occasionally, until the apricots have swollen and the sauce thickened. Spoon the apricots and the lovely sticky sauce into two serving bowls. Top each one with yogurt and walnuts, then serve.

MIDWEEK LIFESAVERS

My midweek lifesavers are all you need to know for those crucial moments in life when you get in late from work and want to eat immediately. No faffing around, these recipes are fast, fresh and furious. Try my heavenly Cambodian Seafood Amok, a coconut curry that can be made in just 15 minutes, or my Little South Island Pork Salad which is made with juicy orange pieces and crunchy fennel, flavoured with Chinese five-spice powder and chilli flakes. This chapter is also home to the mighty Bosporus Burger, a succulent beef burger flavoured with spices and served with blue cheese. This epic creation takes only 15 minutes to make, so you'll never be caught out hungry again. Most recipes in this chapter take 20 minutes or less to prepare and the longest takes only 25 minutes.

Goan Cinnamon & Mint Chicken Curry SERVES **2**   READY IN **20 MINUTES**

This classic Goan dish is one of my favourite curries ever. It's vibrant in colour and fresh tasting, but the best thing is that it's so simple to make. Bung everything into a blender to make a killer sauce, fry the chicken, pour over the sauce and cook for a few minutes. What could be simpler?

120g/4¼oz/scant ⅔ cup basmati rice
2 green chillies
3 garlic cloves
2 large handfuls of coriander leaves and stalks

1 large handful of mint leaves
½ tsp ground cinnamon
½ tsp freshly ground black pepper
1 tsp sugar
1½ tsp Worcestershire sauce
1cm/½in piece fresh root ginger

1 lime
300g/10½oz boneless, skinless chicken thighs
1 tbsp groundnut oil
sea salt

COOK THE RICE in boiling water for 10–12 minutes until soft, or as directed on the packet. Drain in a colander, then cover the rice with a clean tea towel while still in the colander, and leave to one side.

MEANWHILE, CUT THE TOP off each chilli and roll the chilli between your hands to deseed it, then chuck them both into a blender or food processor. Peel the garlic and add it to the blender with the coriander leaves and stalks, mint, cinnamon, black pepper, sugar, Worcestershire sauce and a good pinch of salt. Peel and add the ginger, then squeeze in the juice from the lime and add 100ml/3½fl oz/generous ⅓ cup water. Blend into a smooth sauce.

SLICE THE CHICKEN into thin strips. Heat the oil in a frying pan over a high heat. Add the chicken and stir-fry for 5–6 minutes until it starts to turn golden brown. Tip in the green sauce and reduce the heat to medium. Pour 100ml/3½fl oz/generous ⅓ cup water into the blender, swill it around and add it to the pan to get every last drop of flavour into the dish. Mix everything together really well and simmer for 5–6 minutes, stirring occasionally, until the chicken is cooked through and tender. Serve with the rice.

Phipp Street Stir-Fry SERVES **2** READY IN **15 MINUTES**

I live on Phipp Street in London, and this stir-fry was invented after a long day working in my kitchen. I mine-swept my almost empty fridge, chopped everything up and stir-fried it with some noodles. The result was this awesome dish. I hope it brings you as much satisfaction as it did me when you need a good feed after a long day and have little time for cooking.

140g/5oz vermicelli rice noodles
2 tbsp groundnut oil
2 lemongrass stalks
2 garlic cloves
1 red chilli
1 baby gem lettuce

2 boneless, skinless chicken thighs
  (about 200g/7oz total weight)
2 tsp fish sauce
1 tbsp light soy sauce
½ lime

COOK THE NOODLES in boiling water for 2–3 minutes until soft, or as directed on the packet. Drain in a colander and drizzle with 1 tablespoon of the oil to prevent the noodles from sticking, then leave to one side.

MEANWHILE, GET EVERYTHING READY to stir-fry. Remove the tough outer leaves from the lemongrass and cut off the ends of the stalks. Peel the garlic and cut the top off the chilli, then chuck the lemongrass, garlic and chilli into a mini food processor, and blend into a paste. Cut the stalk off the lettuce and pick off the leaves. Slice the chicken into very thin strips.

HEAT THE REMAINING OIL in a wok over a high heat until smoking. Add the chicken and stir-fry for 5–6 minutes until golden at the edges. Scoop the spice paste into the wok and stir-fry for another 30 seconds, or until fragrant. Add the lettuce leaves, fish sauce and soy sauce, then squeeze in the juice from the lime. Stir-fry for 1–2 minutes until the lettuce leaves have wilted and the chicken is cooked through. Finally, add the noodles, toss everything together and serve.

Chicken Morita with Avocado Sauce SERVES **2**   READY IN **20 MINUTES**

FOR THE CHICKEN MORITA
120g/4¼oz/scant ⅔ cup
   basmati rice
2 garlic cloves
1 tsp smoked paprika
½ tsp chilli powder

2 tbsp sun-dried tomato paste
1 tsp tamarind paste
¼ tsp sugar
2 tbsp olive oil
2 skinless chicken breasts
sea salt

FOR THE AVOCADO SAUCE
1 avocado
1 lime
100g/3½oz/heaped ⅓ cup yogurt
1 small handful of coriander leaves

PREHEAT THE GRILL to high. Cook the rice in boiling water for 10–12 minutes until soft, or as directed on the packet. Drain in a colander, then cover the rice with a clean tea towel while still in the colander, and leave to one side.

MEANWHILE, PEEL THE GARLIC, then put it into a mini food processor, and add the paprika, chilli powder, sun-dried tomato paste, tamarind paste, sugar, 1 tablespoon of the olive oil and a good pinch of salt, and grind into a smooth paste.

LAY THE CHICKEN BREASTS on a chopping board and, using a rolling pin, bash them out until they are about 1.5cm/⅝in thick. Prick the chicken all over with a fork, then rub the paste all over both sides. Put the chicken on to a grill rack and grill for 7–8 minutes until golden on one side.

WHILE THE CHICKEN COOKS, cut the avocado in half and remove the stone using a knife. Scoop the flesh out with a spoon and put it into a blender or food processor. Squeeze in the juice from ½ lime and add the yogurt, coriander, the remaining oil and a good pinch of salt. Blend into a smooth paste, then tip into a serving bowl. Cover and leave to one side. Cut the remaining lime half into 2 wedges.

TURN THE HALF-COOKED CHICKEN over and grill for another 7–8 minutes until cooked through and tender. Serve the chicken with a wedge of lime and the cooked rice, and add the avocado sauce at the table.

Great Eastern Duck Salad SERVES **2** READY IN **25 MINUTES**

1 tbsp olive oil
2 duck breasts (about 165g/5¾oz
  each)
350g/12oz watermelon
½ red chilli
½ lime
2 tbsp hoisin sauce

1 tsp light soy sauce
¼ tsp Chinese five-spice powder
75g/2½oz/2½ cups watercress
1 handful of mint leaves
55g/2oz/heaped ⅓ cup cashew nuts
sea salt

HEAT THE OIL in a frying pan over a high heat. Meanwhile, score the fat on the duck breasts and season both sides with salt. Carefully put the duck in the hot pan, skin-side down, and reduce the heat to medium. Cook for 8–10 minutes until the skin is really crispy.

WHILE THE DUCK COOKS, peel the watermelon and cut it into bite-sized pieces, removing any obvious pips as you go. Chuck the watermelon into a large mixing bowl and leave to one side.

TURN THE CRISPY DUCK over and cook for another 8–10 minutes until beautifully tender and pink in the centre, then remove from the heat.

DESEED AND FINELY SLICE THE CHILLI while the duck finishes cooking. Put it in the mixing bowl with the melon and squeeze over the juice from the lime.

POUR OUT ANY EXCESS FAT from the cooked duck. Add the hoisin sauce, soy sauce and Chinese five-spice powder to the pan, and mix well. Remove the duck breasts from the pan, slice them into thick pieces and leave to one side. Put the watercress, mint and cashew nuts in the bowl with the watermelon, then toss everything together. Serve the salad with the beautiful duck slices, with the juices from the pan spooned over.

Oaxaca Tostadas SERVES **2** READY IN **15 MINUTES**

My *tostadas* were inspired by the wonderful giant *tostadas* of the Central Market in the city of Oaxaca in Mexico. They are completely delicious – you taste hot and cold, crunchy and smooth, spicy and mild, salty and sour in every bite. And, as they only take 15 minutes to make, they are a real midweek lifesaver.

2 tbsp olive oil
2 large tortillas
1 red onion
2 garlic cloves
200g/7oz chorizo, in one piece

2 ripe avocados
1 green chilli
8 spring onions
1 handful of coriander leaves
1½ limes

1 tomato
55g/2oz Gruyère cheese
a pinch of smoked paprika
sea salt

PREHEAT THE GRILL TO HIGH. Meanwhile, brush 1 tablespoon of the oil over both sides of each tortilla. Put them on to a grill rack and grill for 30 seconds–1 minute on each side until crispy and golden at the edges. Remove from the grill and put on to serving plates.

PEEL THE RED ONION AND GARLIC, then slice the onion and roughly chop the garlic and chorizo. Heat the remaining oil in a frying pan over a medium heat and chuck in the sliced and chopped ingredients. Mix well and cook for 5–6 minutes, stirring occasionally, until golden.

MEANWHILE, CUT THE AVOCADOS in half and remove the stones using a knife. Scoop the flesh out with a spoon and put it into a mini food processor or blender. Cut the top off the chilli and trim the spring onions, then add both ingredients to the food processor with the coriander and a pinch of salt. Squeeze in the juice from ½ lime and blend into a rough paste.

FINELY SLICE THE TOMATO, grate the cheese and cut the remaining lime into quarters. Divide the avocado mixture between the 2 tortillas and spread evenly over, using a knife. Top with the tomato slices, hot chorizo and onion, and scatter over the cheese. Give both tostadas a dusting of smoked paprika and serve with lime wedges.

TINY TABLES, MOTORBIKES & BUN CHA

When I arrived in Hanoi I was struck by the madness of the place. The air was sticky, people actually wore conical hats, smoky food stalls lined the streets and an army of predatory motorbikes circled the roads like angry bulls at Pamplona.

Once I had plucked up the courage to cross a road (which was only after watching an old lady fearlessly stride to the other side), I was able to sample the many culinary delights of the city. Perfectly barbecued meats, grilled fish, peppered stir-fries and fragrant soups – it had it all, with fishy, hot, salty and sour flavours beautifully balanced in every bite.

Eating in Hanoi means street food – and it was everywhere. A few stalls had evolved into restaurants, but on the whole you eat out on the curb, crouched at tiny tables. One lunchtime, I visited a packed street stall and squeezed on to a tiny chair, literally in the road, to slurp the lunchtime soup special, *bun cha*. It was amazing – the wonderfully salty soup was spiked with black pepper and served with tender grilled pork. The table came laden with little dishes of rice noodles, herbs and chillies to add to your bowl. This fast-food glory summed up all that was triumphant about Vietnamese food.

Vietnamese Bun Cha SERVES **2** READY IN **20 MINUTES**

FOR THE SOUP
500ml/17fl oz/2 cups chicken
   stock
6 black peppercorns
2 star anise
2.5cm/1in cinnamon stick
2 tsp sugar
3 tbsp fish sauce
2 lemongrass stalks

½ lime
140g/5oz vermicelli rice noodles

FOR THE PORK BURGERS
1 small handful of coriander leaves
1 small handful of mint leaves
120g/4¼oz minced pork
1 tsp fish sauce
1 tsp groundnut oil

TO SERVE
4 spring onions
½ red chilli
½ lime
140g/5oz/1½ cups bean sprouts
1 large handful of coriander leaves
1 large handful of mint leaves

POUR THE STOCK and 500ml/17fl oz/2 cups water into a saucepan and add the peppercorns, star anise, cinnamon stick, sugar and fish sauce. Bash the fat ends of the lemongrass stalks with a spoon, snap them in half and add them to the stock. Squeeze in the juice from the lime, mix well and bring to the boil over a medium heat.

MEANWHILE, ADD THE NOODLES to a pan of boiling water and leave to stand for 3 minutes, or as directed on the packet. Drain in a colander and refresh under cold water, then drain again. Leave them in the colander to drain.

CHOP THE HERBS for the pork burgers and put them into a large bowl. Add the pork and fish sauce and mix well. Heat the oil in a frying pan over a medium heat. Meanwhile, divide the pork into 4 and flatten into mini burger shapes. Fry the burgers for 3 minutes on each side, or until golden and cooked through.

WHILE THE PORK IS COOKING, trim the spring onions, then cut each in half and then into thin strips. Deseed the chilli, then slice it finely. Cut the lime into 2 pieces.

DIVIDE THE NOODLES and bean sprouts between two large serving bowls, and put 2 pork burgers into each bowl. Scatter half the spring onions and the chilli over each bowl, then top with the lime and the herbs. Remove the spices from the stock and divide the hot, fragrant soup between the two bowls. Serve immediately.

Little South Island Pork Salad SERVES **2**   READY IN **20 MINUTES**

This dish sums up why eating real Chinese food is such a pleasure. No nuclear-red gloopy sauce, not a tinned pineapple chunk in sight – just simple, fresh, clean flavours that all work superbly together and take minutes to make. The crunchy fennel and sweet carrot soak up all the richness of the stir-fried pork and the delicious flavours of the tart dressing. This is how Chinese food should be!

FOR THE PORK SALAD
1 tbsp groundnut oil
350g/12oz minced pork
½ tsp Chinese five-spice powder
½ tsp crushed chilli flakes

1 tbsp light soy sauce
1 orange
1 fennel bulb
1 carrot
100g/3½oz frisée lettuce

FOR THE GINGER DRESSING
1½ tbsp cider vinegar
2 tsp light soy sauce
1cm/½in piece fresh root ginger

HEAT A WOK over a high heat until smoking. Pour in the oil, swirl it round and then add the pork. Stir-fry for 5–6 minutes until the edges of the pork start to catch and become golden.

SPRINKLE IN THE CHINESE FIVE-SPICE POWDER and chilli flakes, then add the soy sauce. Continue to stir-fry for 30 seconds, then remove from the heat and leave to one side.

USING A SHARP KNIFE, cut the top and bottom off the orange, and stand it up on your chopping board. Carefully slice the skin off in sections, cutting from top to bottom. Remove any remaining pith, then cut out the juicy pieces of orange from the membrane and put them in a mixing bowl. Squeeze in the juice from the membrane.

FINELY SLICE THE FENNEL and add it to the bowl with the orange. Peel the carrot and grate it, using the coarse setting on a grater, into the bowl. Pour in the cider vinegar and soy sauce for the dressing, then peel and grate in the ginger, using the fine setting. Put the lettuce leaves and cooked pork, along with all the lovely juices, into the mixing bowl with the salad. Toss everything together and serve.

Mr Wong's Hunan Lamb SERVES **2** READY IN **20 MINUTES**

This dish is all about the big spices of Hunanese cooking. A fiery paste made from dried chillies, Sichuan pepper, ginger and spring onions coats the delicate lamb cutlets and turns them into something fierce. The sweetness of the lamb handles all the big flavours, and the delicate pak choi, soy and orange stir-fry absorbs some of the heat.

FOR THE LAMB
2 dried red chillies
1 tsp Sichuan pepper
1cm/½in piece fresh root ginger
5 spring onions

2 tbsp groundnut oil
6 lamb cutlets (about 500g/1lb 2oz total weight)
sea salt

FOR THE PAK CHOI AND ORANGE STIR-FRY
200g/7oz pak choi
1 tbsp groundnut oil
1 tbsp soy sauce
½ orange

PREHEAT THE GRILL to high. Meanwhile, put the chillies, Sichuan pepper and a pinch of salt into a mini food processor, and blend into a coarse powder. Peel the ginger and trim the spring onions, then add them to the food processor, and add the oil. Blend into a rough paste.

LIGHTLY SCORE both sides of the lamb cutlets in a crisscross pattern and put them in a mixing bowl. Tip in the spice paste and mix everything together really well so that the paste completely covers the lamb. Put the lamb on a grill rack and grill for 5–6 minutes on each side until golden on the outside and pink and juicy in the centre.

WHILE THE LAMB COOKS, cut the pak choi lengthways into quarters. Heat a wok over a high heat until smoking and pour in the oil. Chuck in the pak choi and stir-fry for 2 minutes, then add the soy sauce and squeeze in the juice from the orange. Continue to stir-fry for 30 seconds, then reduce the heat to low and cook for 3–4 minutes until tender. Serve the stir-fry with the lamb.

Griddled Aubergine with Lamb, Mint & Feta SERVES **2**   READY IN **15 MINUTES**

This is my express version of a classic Eastern Mediterranean stuffed-aubergine dish. I griddle the aubergine, which is the fastest way to cook it, and top it with stir-fried lamb. The final addition of mint and feta completes the dish with the fresh and salty flavours it needs.

1 large aubergine
3 tbsp olive oil
2 bay leaves
300g/10½oz minced lamb
1¼ tsp ground allspice
½ tsp ground cinnamon

2 garlic cloves
300g/10½oz/scant 1¼ cups tomato passata
60g/2¼oz feta cheese
1 small handful of mint leaves

sea salt and freshly ground black pepper

TO SERVE
green salad

HEAT A GRIDDLE over a high heat until smoking. Meanwhile, cut the aubergine lengthways into 1cm/½in slices and put them in a mixing bowl. Add 2 tablespoons of the oil and a good pinch of salt and pepper. Mix everything together really well so that both sides of the aubergine slices are coated in the oil. Griddle for 2½–3 minutes on each side until charred and tender. Divide between two serving plates and leave to one side.

WHILE THE AUBERGINE COOKS, heat the remaining oil in a frying pan over a medium heat. Add the bay leaves and cook for 5 seconds until fragrant. Add the lamb, allspice, cinnamon and a good pinch of salt and pepper. Peel and crush in the garlic, turn the heat up to high and stir-fry for 3–4 minutes until the lamb is golden.

POUR IN THE PASSATA and mix well. Reduce the heat to medium and cook for 3–4 minutes, stirring occasionally, until the lamb is cooked through and the sauce has thickened. To serve the dish, spoon the lamb over the griddled aubergine slices and crumble over the feta cheese. Scatter over the mint leaves and serve with a green salad.

Taiwanese Beef Noodle Stir-Fry SERVES **2** READY IN **15 MINUTES**

140g/5oz medium egg noodles
2½ tbsp groundnut oil
225g/8oz sirloin steak
1 red chilli
4 spring onions
4 garlic cloves

5mm/¼in piece fresh root ginger
70g/2½oz mangetout
½ tsp freshly ground black pepper
½ tsp sugar
2 tbsp soy sauce

COOK THE NOODLES in boiling water for 4–5 minutes until soft, or as directed on the packet. Drain in a colander and drizzle with 1 tablespoon of the oil to prevent the noodles from sticking. Using a pair of scissors, cut the noodles a few at a time to break them up, then leave to one side. This will help them mix quicker in the wok.

MEANWHILE, PREPARE ALL THE INGREDIENTS for the stir-fry. Finely slice the beef into very thin strips. Cut the top off the chilli, then finely slice the chilli. Trim the spring onions and cut into 2.5cm/1in pieces. Peel and cut the garlic cloves in half lengthways. Peel the ginger, then slice it into thin strips.

HEAT A WOK over a high heat until smoking. Pour in the remaining oil and add the chilli, spring onions, garlic and ginger, then stir-fry for 30 seconds until beautifully aromatic. Add the beef and continue to stir-fry for 2 minutes, then add the mangetout, black pepper and sugar.

CONTINUE TO STIR-FRY for 1–2 minutes until everything has taken on a lovely golden colour and the beef is cooked through. Transfer the cooked noodles to the hot wok and pour in the soy sauce. Mix well and serve.

Beef Chilli & Mint Stir-Fry SERVES **2** READY IN **15 MINUTES**

Never one to miss a meal, I ordered my lunch to go as I was leaving my hotel in Laos to head to the airport and back to Blighty. I was literally eating my food as I walked to the taxi. Boy, am I glad that I am greedy. Lunch was superb – a simple beef stir-fry with chilli, garlic and a few peanuts, which was lifted somewhere new with a handful of mint leaves. The mint was a superb addition to a classic South-east Asian stir-fry and probably even worth missing a flight for.

140g/5oz fine egg noodles
2½ tbsp groundnut oil
2 garlic cloves
2.5cm/1in piece fresh root ginger
1 red chilli

2 sirloin steaks (about 120g/4¼oz each)
55g/2oz/heaped ⅓ cup peanuts
1 tsp rice wine vinegar
1 tbsp light soy sauce

3 tbsp oyster sauce
150g/5½oz/1⅔ cups bean sprouts
1 handful of small mint leaves

COOK THE NOODLES in boiling water for for 4–5 minutes until soft, or as directed on the packet. Drain in a colander and drizzle with ½ tablespoon of the oil to prevent the noodles from sticking, then leave to one side. Meanwhile, peel and finely slice the garlic and ginger. Cut the top off the chilli, then slice the chilli. Trim the fat off the beef and slice into strips about 2mm/⅟₁₆in thick.

HEAT A WOK over a high heat and add 1 tablespoon of the oil. Put in the peanuts and stir-fry for 1 minute or until golden. Remove with a slotted spoon and transfer to kitchen paper to drain. Tip the oil out of the wok and return the wok to a high heat. Once smoking, add the remaining oil and the beef. Leave to sear for 40 seconds, then stir-fry for 30 seconds to take on some colour. Chuck in the garlic, ginger and chilli, and continue to stir-fry for 2–3 minutes until golden.

POUR IN THE RICE WINE VINEGAR, soy sauce and oyster sauce, and mix well. Add the bean sprouts and continue to stir-fry for 1–2 minutes until the bean sprouts are just tender but still have a little bite. Turn off the heat, then tip in the peanuts and add the mint. Give it a final mix, then add the noodles, stir and serve.

The Bosporus Burger SERVES **2** READY IN **15 MINUTES**

1 small handful of parsley leaves
1 tsp paprika
2 tsp ground cumin
½ tsp ground ginger
½ tsp chilli powder
300g/10½oz minced beef
1 tbsp olive oil

55g/2oz blue cheese
4 tbsp mayonnaise
¼ lemon
2 burger buns
1 handful of mixed lettuce leaves
sea salt

FINELY CHOP THE PARSLEY and chuck it into a large mixing bowl. Add the paprika, cumin, ground ginger, chilli powder, minced beef and a really good pinch of salt. Mix everything together really well – I find that squeezing the mix together in your fists works best.

DIVIDE THE BEEF MIXTURE into 2 portions and flatten each one into a burger. Push your thumb into the top of each burger to create a little indent, which will help the burgers to cook evenly.

HEAT THE OIL in a frying pan over a high heat and add the burgers, indented side facing up. Cook for 4 minutes, then turn the burgers over, reduce the heat to medium-low and cook for another 3 minutes. Top each burger with half the blue cheese and cook for 1 minute, or until the burgers are cooked through and wonderfully juicy and the cheese has just melted.

WHILE THE BURGERS COOK, put the mayonnaise in a mixing bowl and squeeze in the juice from the lemon. Add a pinch of salt and mix well. Split the burger buns in half and spread the mayonnaise evenly over the base half of each. Divide the lettuce leaves over the mayo'd buns. Add the cooked burgers, put the top of the buns on the burgers and tuck in straight away.

Salmon Bibimbap SERVES **2** READY IN **20 MINUTES**

Bibimbap is a classic Korean rice dish. Cooked rice is put into a boiling-hot stone bowl, so that it forms a crunchy base. Different toppings – salmon, eggs, vegetables or pork – are added, and the dish is served with kimchi and a soy-based sauce. To get that crispy base, make sure, when you cook my salmon version, that the pan is really hot before you add the cooked rice.

FOR THE RICE
120g/4¼oz/scant ⅔ cup jasmine
   rice
1cm/½in piece fresh root ginger
3 spring onions
1 tbsp light soy sauce
1 tbsp cider vinegar

FOR THE SALMON AND EGGS
2 tbsp olive oil
2 boneless, skinless salmon fillets
2 eggs
1 tsp sesame seeds

FOR THE CHILLI DRESSING
1 garlic clove
4 tbsp chilli sauce
1 tbsp soy sauce
1 tbsp cider vinegar
1 tsp sesame oil

COOK THE RICE in boiling water for 10–12 minutes until soft, or as directed on the packet. Drain in a colander, return to the pan, then cover and leave to one side. Meanwhile, heat 1 tablespoon of the oil for the salmon in a frying pan over a medium heat and add the salmon. Cook for 2 minutes, then turn, reduce the heat to low and cook for 1½–2 minutes until cooked on the outside and pink in the centre. Leave to one side.

WHILE THE SALMON COOKS, peel the garlic for the dressing. Put all the dressing ingredients into a mini food processor, and blend until smooth. Leave to one side.

PEEL THE GINGER for the rice and trim the spring onions, then finely chop them both and put them into the pan with the cooked rice. Add the soy sauce and cider vinegar, then mix together really well using a fork. Cover and leave to one side.

HEAT THE REMAINING OIL in a large frying pan over a high heat and add the rice, spreading it evenly, then create two wells, using a spoon, and crack in the eggs. Cover and cook for 2–3 minutes until the whites have set, the yolks are runny and the rice has started to brown underneath. Divide the rice and eggs between two plates. Flake over the salmon and scatter over the sesame seeds. Drizzle with the dressing and serve.

Cambodian Seafood Amok SERVES 2 READY IN **15 MINUTES**

FOR THE RICE NOODLES
100g/3½oz medium rice noodles
1 tbsp groundnut oil

FOR THE AMOK CURRY PASTE
1cm/½in piece fresh root ginger
2 lemongrass stalks
3 garlic cloves
½ tsp turmeric

2 dried red chillies
½ tsp freshly ground black pepper
½ tsp sugar
30g/1oz/scant ¼ cup peanuts
2 tbsp groundnut oil

FOR THE SEAFOOD CURRY
250ml/9fl oz/1 cup coconut cream
1 tbsp fish sauce

½ lime
2 haddock fillets (about 150g/5½oz
  each)
115g/4oz prepared raw mixed
  seafood, such as mussels, king
  prawns and squid rings
1 small handful of coriander leaves

COOK THE RICE NOODLES in boiling water for 4–5 minutes until soft, or as directed on the packet. Drain in a colander and drizzle with the oil to prevent the noodles from sticking. Cover and leave to one side.

MEANWHILE, TO MAKE THE CURRY PASTE, peel the ginger, then remove the tough outer leaves from the lemongrass and cut off the ends of the stalks. Peel the garlic. Put all the curry paste ingredients into a mini food processor, and blend into a smooth paste, adding a little water if necessary.

HEAT A LARGE WOK over a medium heat and add the curry paste. Stir-fry for 30 seconds, or until fragrant. Pour in the coconut cream and fish sauce for the seafood curry, squeeze in the juice from the lime and mix everything together really well. Bring the amok sauce to the boil while you prepare the fish.

CHOP THE HADDOCK into bite-sized pieces. Chuck them into the hot amok sauce and add the mixed seafood. Gently mix everything together, reduce the heat to low and simmer gently for 5–6 minutes, stirring occasionally, until the fish starts to flake and the seafood is cooked through.

WHILE THE AMOK COOKS, roughly tear the coriander. Serve the curry with the rice noodles, topped with the coriander.

Crayfish, Pink Grapefruit & Glass Noodle Salad SERVES **2** READY IN **15 MINUTES**

FOR THE GLASS NOODLE SALAD
140g/5oz vermicelli rice noodles
1 pink grapefruit
2 spring onions
30g/1oz pea shoots
150g/5½oz cooked, peeled
    crayfish tails

1 small handful of basil leaves
1 small handful of mint leaves
2 tbsp pumpkin seeds

**FOR THE LEMONGRASS
    DRESSING**
2 lemongrass stalks
2 limes
¼ tsp chilli powder
2 tsp sugar
1 tbsp olive oil

PUT THE NOODLES into a heatproof bowl and cover with boiling water. Cover and leave to one side for 2–3 minutes to soften. Once soft, drain in a colander and rinse with cold water. Drain again and squeeze out any excess water with your hands so that they are really dry. Leave to one side.

MAKE THE DRESSING while the noodles soften. Remove the tough outer leaves from the lemongrass and cut off the ends of the stalks. Starting at the fatter end, roughly slice each lemongrass stalk into rings. You should see a purple band in the rings. Stop slicing when there are no more purple bands, then discard the rest of the lemongrass, as it will be too tough to eat.

GIVE THE LEMONGRASS SLICES a quick blast in a mini food processor until they are very finely chopped, then tip them into a large mixing bowl. Squeeze the juice from the limes into the bowl with the lemongrass and add the chilli powder, sugar and oil. Whisk everything together to get the flavours going.

USING A SHARP KNIFE, cut the top and bottom off the grapefruit, then stand it up on your chopping board. Carefully slice the skin off in sections, cutting from top to bottom. Remove any remaining pith, then cut out the juicy pieces of grapefruit from the membrane and put them into the bowl with the dressing. Squeeze in the juice from the membrane. Trim and finely slice the spring onions, then add them to the bowl. Chuck in the pea shoots, crayfish, basil, mint and cooked noodles. Toss everything together well. Serve with the pumpkin seeds scattered over the top.

Warm East-Med Aubergine & Tomato Salad SERVES **2**   READY IN **15 MINUTES**

5 tbsp olive oil
2 tsp dried mint
2 aubergines
½ red onion
1½ lemons
½ red chilli
100g/3½oz/heaped ⅔ cup cherry
   tomatoes

75g/2½oz/scant ⅔ cup pitted black
   olives
2 large handfuls of parsley leaves
½ tsp sumac
1 tsp ground cumin
2 tbsp pine nuts (optional)
sea salt and freshly ground black
   pepper

PREHEAT THE GRILL to high. Meanwhile, put 3 tablespoons of the oil,
1½ teaspoons of the mint and a good pinch of salt in a mixing bowl, and mix well.
Slice the aubergines into 5mm/¼in rings and brush both sides with the seasoned oil.
Put the aubergines on to a grill rack and grill for 5–6 minutes until golden on one side.

WHILE THE AUBERGINES COOK, peel and finely slice the onion, then chuck it in
a large mixing bowl. Squeeze over the juice from the lemons, add a pinch of salt and mix
well. Finely chop the chilli and cut the cherry tomatoes in half. Put them in the bowl
with the onion.

WHEN THE AUBERGINES HAVE COOKED on one side, turn them over and grill
for another 5–6 minutes until golden on the other side and tender in the centre.

TEAR THE OLIVES and rip the parsley leaves into the mixing bowl with the salad.
Add the remaining oil and mint, and the sumac, cumin and a good pinch of black
pepper. Toss everything together. Put the cooked aubergines in the bowl with the salad
and mix everything together really well. Serve the salad with the pine nuts, if using,
scattered over the top.

Heather's Moroccan Paprika & Garlic Lentils SERVES **2** READY IN **20 MINUTES**

I stayed with Heather in her beautiful home just outside Marrakesh for a few days of sunshine and cooking. She taught me how to make loads of amazing dishes, including the classic cold Moroccan lentil salad. It was delicious, and I loved it hot straight out of the pan. She used a beautiful expression to describe when the dish was ready, "When the lentils have 'drunk all the water' it's done." Although my version is a little different, you can tell when it's ready – when the lentils have "drunk all the water" and the sauce is beautifully thick, it's ready for you to add the lemon and herbs and then to tuck in.

1 onion
4 garlic cloves
2 tbsp olive oil
2 bay leaves
800g/1lb 12oz/3 cups tinned
   green lentils

3 tbsp tomato purée
1¼ tsp paprika
2 tsp ground cumin
1½ tsp freshly ground black pepper
1 tsp sugar
1 large handful of parsley leaves

½ lemon
sea salt

TO SERVE
extra virgin olive oil

PEEL AND FINELY CHOP the onion and garlic, then put them in a large saucepan, along with the olive oil and bay leaves. Heat over a medium heat and cook for 5–6 minutes, stirring occasionally, until soft.

MEANWHILE, DRAIN AND RINSE the lentils, and leave to one side. Once the onion is soft, add the tomato purée, paprika, cumin, black pepper, sugar, lentils and a good pinch of salt. Pour in 320ml/11fl oz/scant 1⅓ cups hot water and mix well. Bring to the boil and cook for 5–6 minutes, stirring frequently, until the lentils have warmed through and the sauce is really thick.

WHILE THE LENTILS COOK, finely chop the parsley. Add the chopped parsley to the pan with the cooked lentils and squeeze in the juice from the lemon. Mix well and serve with a drizzle of your fanciest olive oil.

Indian Cauliflower Soup SERVES **2** READY IN **15 MINUTES**

This is such an awesome soup. It's rich, thick and packed with flavour. The ground spices provide a background layer of warmth, but it's the temper that really packs a punch. Tempering a dish means simply frying some spices in hot oil and pouring them into the dish at the end of cooking. It adds an extra layer of flavour, and it really brings the food to life.

FOR THE SOUP
1 small cauliflower
185ml/6fl oz/¾ cup vegetable
   stock
400ml/14fl oz/generous 1½ cups
   coconut milk
2 tsp garam masala

½ tsp turmeric
¼ tsp chilli powder
400g/14oz/2 cups tinned butter
   beans
½ lime
sea salt

FOR THE TEMPER
1 onion
2 garlic cloves
2 tbsp groundnut oil
2 large pinches of dried
   curry leaves

USING YOUR HANDS, break up the cauliflower into very small pieces straight into a saucepan. Cover with boiling water and cook over a high heat for 6–8 minutes until tender.

MEANWHILE, POUR THE STOCK and coconut milk into a saucepan, and add the garam masala, turmeric, chilli powder and a good pinch of salt. Mix well and bring to the boil over a high heat. Reduce the heat to low and simmer gently. While the soup simmers, peel and finely chop the onion and garlic for the temper. Drain the butter beans in a colander and rinse with cold water.

ONCE THE CAULIFLOWER IS TENDER, drain, using the colander containing the beans. Tip both into the saucepan with the soup. Remove the pan from the heat and blend until smooth, using a hand blender or food processor. Return the soup to a low heat and simmer gently, stirring occasionally, while you make the temper.

TO MAKE THE TEMPER, heat the oil in a frying pan over a high heat and add the onion and garlic. Stir-fry for 2–3 minutes until golden. Remove from the heat. Rub the curry leaves between your hands so that the leaves break up into the frying pan. Tip the temper into the soup and squeeze in the juice from the lime. Mix well and serve.

Nice & Easy

In this chapter all the recipes take a really chilled-out approach to cooking for friends and family. I am talking about great food that is quite simply nice and easy to make. You can do any of these recipes armed with a glass of wine and not miss out on any of the fun, because they are all ready in 45 minutes or less. My Sumac Chicken with Black Gremolata & Tomato Salad is effortless and ready in 45 minutes. Amish's Gujarati Vegetable Curry, enriched with cashew nuts and served with rice and chickpeas, is utterly sublime and takes only 35 minutes to make. Or my Mexican Sea Bream with Roasted Lemon Courgettes & Spicy Lime Seasoning has all the flavours to blow you away, but it only takes a cool 40 minutes to cook from start to finish.

Korean Braised Chicken with Rice Noodles SERVES **4**   READY IN **35 MINUTES**

All Korean food should have a balance of five colours – black, white, yellow, green and red. Here, the black is from the soy, the white from the chicken, yellow from the noodles, green from the coriander and red from the chillies.

550g/1lb 4oz boneless, skinless chicken thighs
70ml/2¼fl oz/generous ¼ cup soy sauce
1 tbsp oyster sauce
3 tbsp rice wine or dry white wine
½ tbsp sesame oil
2 tbsp brown sugar

½ tsp ground ginger
½ tsp freshly ground black pepper
2 dried red chillies
4 garlic cloves
1 onion
1 carrot
1 courgette
200g/7oz vermicelli rice noodles

100ml/3½fl oz/generous ⅓ cup chicken stock
2 spring onions
½ red chilli
1 small handful of coriander leaves

CHUCK THE CHICKEN in a large, shallow flameproof casserole and pour over the soy sauce, oyster sauce, rice wine, sesame oil, brown sugar, ground ginger and black pepper. Crack open the dried chillies and throw them into the casserole, then peel and crush in the garlic. Mix everything together really well and heat over a medium heat.

PEEL AND ROUGHLY SLICE the onion, then peel the carrot. Chop the carrot and courgette into matchsticks. Put the vegetables in the casserole with the chicken and mix together. It will look a little dry at this stage, but don't worry – lots of lovely juices will come from the chicken and vegetables. Bring to the boil, cover and reduce the heat to low. Simmer gently for 15 minutes, or until the chicken is just cooked through.

MEANWHILE, PUT THE NOODLES in a large mixing bowl, cover with boiling water and leave to one side to soften for about 10 minutes. Pour the stock into a small saucepan and heat gently over a medium-low heat. Once the chicken is cooked, drain the noodles in a colander and add them to the casserole in four little piles. Pour over the stock, then cover and cook for another 10 minutes to allow the noodles to soak up the sauce. Trim and finely slice the spring onions and red chilli, then roughly tear the coriander. Scatter over the dish and serve.

Roast Spatchcocked Chicken with Chimichurri & Rice & Black Bean Salad SERVES 4 READY IN **45 MINUTES**

FOR THE CHICKEN
1 chicken, 1.4kg/3lb 2oz
1 tbsp olive oil
sea salt and freshly ground black
    pepper

**FOR THE RICE AND BLACK
    BEAN SALAD**
200g/7oz/1 cup brown rice
235g/8½oz/generous 1 cup tinned
    black beans
½ red onion

1 large handful of mint leaves
1 large handful of parsley leaves
2 tbsp sherry vinegar
100g/3½oz/⅔ cup cashew nuts

FOR THE CHIMICHURRI
1 red chilli
½ red onion
2 garlic cloves
1 large handful of parsley leaves
1 tomato
2 tsp dried oregano

2 tsp ground cumin
1 tsp smoked paprika
4 tbsp olive oil
4 tbsp sherry vinegar

FOR THE LEAF SALAD
120g/4¼oz mixed salad leaves
½ lemon
1 tbsp olive oil

PREHEAT THE OVEN to 220°C/425°F/Gas 7. Put the chicken on to a chopping board breast-side down. Using a pair of kitchen scissors, cut along either side of the spine from the neck to the rear cavity and remove it. Pull the two sides apart so that the chicken starts to open out, turn it over, breast-side up, and press down hard on each side so that the chicken flattens out. This will allow it to roast quickly and evenly.

LAY THE SPATCHCOCKED CHICKEN on a rack over an ovenproof grill pan or a roasting tin, rub over the oil and season with salt and pepper. Roast for 35 minutes, or until the chicken is cooked through and the juices run clear when the thickest part of the thigh is pierced with the tip of a sharp knife.

MEANWHILE, COOK THE RICE for the rice and black bean salad in boiling water for 20–25 minutes until soft, or as directed on the packet.

TO MAKE THE CHIMICHURRI, cut the top off the chilli and roll the chilli between your hands to deseed it. Peel the onion and garlic. Put all the ingredients for the chimichurri into a food processor or blender with 100ml/3½fl oz/generous ⅓ cup water and a little salt, and pulse into a coarse paste. Pour into a serving bowl, then cover with cling film and leave to one side to allow the flavours to develop.

DRAIN AND RINSE THE BEANS for the rice and black bean salad, and put in a large serving bowl. Peel the red onion, then put it into a blender or mini food processor, and add the mint and parsley. Pulse until finely chopped, then add to the bowl with the beans. Spoon in one-third of the chimichurri and add the sherry vinegar, then season with salt.

HEAT A SMALL FRYING PAN over a medium heat and add the cashew nuts. Toast them for 5–6 minutes until lightly golden, shaking the pan frequently to stop them from burning. Remove from the heat and leave to one side to cool.

TIP THE SALAD LEAVES into a plastic food bag. Squeeze the juice from the lemon into the bag and add the oil. Hold two sides of the bag together, shake well and tip into a serving bowl.

PUT THE ROASTED CHICKEN on to a carving board. Drain the rice in a colander and immediately refresh under cold water. Drain well and shake the colander to remove as much water as possible, then add the rice to the bowl with the beans. Add the cashew nuts and toss everything together so that the rice is completely coated with the dressing. Serve the lovely hot chicken with the rice and bean salad, the leaf salad and the chimichurri.

Sumac Chicken with Black Gremolata & Tomato Salad SERVES 4 READY IN **45 MINUTES**

FOR THE SUMAC CHICKEN
3 tbsp olive oil
1.5kg/3lb 5oz chicken thighs
  and drumsticks on the bone
500g/1lb 2oz small new potatoes
1 red onion
1 garlic bulb
1 tbsp sumac
2 tsp dried thyme
sea salt and freshly ground
  black pepper

FOR THE BLACK GREMOLATA
85g/3oz/⅔ cup pitted black olives
1 dried red chilli
¼ tsp sumac
1 large handful of parsley leaves
1 large handful of dill
3 tbsp olive oil
2 tsp best sticky sweet balsamic
  vinegar
½ lemon
55g/2oz/scant ½ cup walnut pieces

FOR THE TOMATO SALAD
300g/10½oz mixed tomatoes,
  such as cherry, vine, baby, plum
2 tbsp best sticky sweet balsamic
  vinegar
2 tbsp olive oil
a pinch of sugar

PREHEAT THE OVEN to 200°C/400°F/Gas 6. Rub a little of the oil over the base of a roasting tin and chuck in the chicken pieces and new potatoes. Peel the onion, cut it into quarters and add it to the chicken. Smash open the garlic bulb and remove 1 clove for the black gremolata, then scatter the rest over the chicken.

SEASON THE CHICKEN with the sumac and thyme, and a good pinch of salt and pepper. Pour over the remaining oil and mix everything together really well. Roast for 35–40 minutes until all the chicken is cooked through and tender, and everything is golden brown.

MEANWHILE, TO MAKE THE GREMOLATA, peel the reserved garlic, then chuck it into a mini food processor or blender, and add the olives, chilli, sumac, parsley, dill, oil, balsamic vinegar and a pinch of salt and pepper. Squeeze in the juice from the lemon and grind into a coarse paste. Tip into a serving bowl and stir in the walnut pieces. Cover and leave to one side to allow those fantastic flavours to intensify.

TO MAKE THE SALAD, cut the tomatoes into different shapes and sizes, and put them in a serving bowl. Pour in the vinegar and olive oil, then season with the sugar, salt and pepper. Toss together. Cover and leave to one side to allow the tomatoes to soak up the seasonings. Serve the chicken with the potatoes, gremolata and the salad.

Five-Spice Pork Belly SERVES **4** READY IN **40 MINUTES**

Mustard is a classic accompaniment to crispy pork belly in Hong Kong – it works well and cuts through the richness of the meat. Get your butcher or supermarket meat-counter assistant to score the fat of the pork belly to help save you loads of preparation time.

FOR THE FIVE-SPICE PORK
1.25kg/2lb 12oz piece pork belly, skin scored
4 tsp Chinese five-spice powder
1 tsp ground Sichuan pepper
sea salt

FOR THE DIPPING SAUCE
3 tbsp soy sauce
1 tbsp rice wine vinegar
2 tbsp clear honey
¼ tsp chilli powder
1 garlic clove

FOR THE RICE AND PAK CHOI
250g/9oz/1¼ cups jasmine rice
200g/7oz pak choi

TO SERVE
85g/3oz/scant ⅓ cup French mustard

PREHEAT THE OVEN to 250°C/500°F/Gas 9. Cut the pork belly into 2 pieces to help it cook quicker, and put both pieces, skin-side up, in a roasting tin. Rub the skin with the Chinese five-spice powder, ground Sichuan pepper and a good pinch of salt. Put it into the oven, reduce the heat to 220°C/425°F/Gas 7 and cook for 30–35 minutes until the pork is cooked through and the skin is madly crispy.

MEANWHILE, MAKE THE DIPPING SAUCE. Pour the soy sauce into a serving bowl and add 2 tablespoons water, the rice wine vinegar and honey. Add the chilli powder, then peel and crush in the garlic. Whisk together, then cover and leave to one side to allow the flavours to develop.

COOK THE RICE in boiling water for 10–12 minutes until soft, or as directed on the packet, then drain in a colander. Pour boiling water into the saucepan to a depth of 2.5cm/1in and heat over a low heat. Put the colander with the rice over the pan and leave to steam gently until you are ready to eat.

WHEN THE PORK HAS COOKED for 25 minutes, cut the pak choi into quarters, then put it into a steamer and steam over a high heat for 5 minutes, or until just tender. Divide the sticky rice into four serving bowls and tip the mustard into a serving dish. Carve the pork and serve with the rice, pak choi, dipping sauce and mustard.

Thai Pork with Noodles & Lemongrass & Lime Dipping Sauce SERVES 4 READY IN 40 MINUTES

FOR THE ROAST PORK
600g/1lb 5oz pork tenderloin
4 garlic cloves
1 tsp freshly ground black pepper
½ tsp sugar
1 tbsp rice wine
2 tsp fish sauce
1 tbsp groundnut oil

FOR THE LEMONGRASS AND LIME DIPPING SAUCE
2 lemongrass stalks
1cm/½in piece fresh root ginger
1 handful of coriander leaves and stalks
½ tsp chilli powder
2 tsp sugar
1 tbsp fish sauce
1½ limes

FOR THE NOODLES
150g/5½oz green beans
200g/7oz medium egg noodles
2 tbsp groundnut oil
1 tbsp fish sauce
½ lime

PREHEAT THE OVEN to 200°C/400°F/Gas 6. Trim the pork and cut it into 10cm/ 4in pieces and prick all over with a fork. Put the pieces of pork into an ovenproof dish, then peel and crush over the garlic. Add the black pepper, sugar, rice wine, fish sauce and oil. Mix everything together well and roast for 30–35 minutes until the pork is just cooked through and tender.

MEANWHILE, TO MAKE THE DIPPING SAUCE, remove the tough outer leaves from the lemongrass and cut off the ends of the stalks. Peel the ginger. Put the lemongrass and ginger into a mini food processor, and add the coriander leaves and stalks, chilli powder, sugar and fish sauce. Squeeze in the juice from the limes and add 4 tablespoons water. Blend into a smooth sauce and pour into a serving bowl. Cover and leave to one side so that all the amazing savoury flavours come together.

CUT THE BEANS for the noodles in half. Cook with the noodles in boiling water for 4–5 minutes until the noodles are soft, or as directed on the packet. Drain and return to the saucepan. Pour in the oil and fish sauce, then squeeze in the juice from the lime. Mix well, cover and leave to one side until the pork is ready. Slice the pork and serve with the noodles and the dipping sauce.

Rana's Keema Shepherd's Pie SERVES **4** READY IN **45 MINUTES**

FOR THE SPICY MASH
750g/1lb 10oz new potatoes
30g/1oz butter
1 tsp garam masala
3 spring onions
1 tbsp olive oil

FOR THE LAMB
1 red onion
2 tbsp groundnut oil

3 cardamom pods
3 large blades of mace
500g/1lb 2oz minced lamb
1 handful of coriander leaves

FOR THE TOMATO SAUCE
2.5cm/1in piece fresh root ginger
4 garlic cloves
100g/3½oz/heaped ⅓ cup tomato
  purée

1½ tsp garam masala
1 tsp chilli powder
½ tsp ground cinnamon
150g/5½oz/scant 1 cup frozen
  peas
sea salt

COOK THE UNPEELED POTATOES in a large pan of boiling water for 15 minutes, or until tender. Meanwhile, prepare the lamb. Peel and finely chop the red onion. Heat the groundnut oil in a large frying pan over a medium heat and add the onion, cardamom pods and mace. Mix well, then add the lamb. Increase the heat to high and stir-fry for 3–4 minutes until the lamb is just cooked through. Reduce the heat to medium and cook for a few minutes, stirring occasionally, while you make the sauce.

TO MAKE THE SAUCE, peel the ginger and garlic, then put both into a mini food processor or blender, and add the tomato purée, garam masala, chilli powder, cinnamon and a good pinch of salt. Blend until smooth. Scoop the sauce into the pan with the lamb and add 150ml/5fl oz/scant ⅔ cup hot water and the peas. Mix well and cover, then reduce the heat to low and simmer gently for 15 minutes, stirring occasionally.

DRAIN THE COOKED POTATOES, then return them to the pan. Mash lightly, so that they start to break up, then add the butter, garam masala and a good pinch of salt. Put the lid on the saucepan. Trim and finely chop the spring onions, then chuck them into the pan and mix everything together well. Cover and leave to one side.

PREHEAT THE GRILL to high and finely chop the coriander for the lamb. When the mince is rich, scatter over the coriander and mix well. Carefully tip the cooked mince into an ovenproof dish and spoon over the spiced potatoes. Drizzle the olive oil over the top and grill for 5 minutes, or until crisped up and golden. Serve.

Lamb with Tarator Sauce, Mashed Potatoes & Tomato & Radish Salad SERVES **4** READY IN **40 MINUTES**

Tarator sauce is a bread sauce with attitude and, served with lamb, makes a classic Middle Eastern combination. It's packed with lemon juice, garlic, pine nuts, cumin and olive oil and it works beautifully with sweet and juicy lamb chops, gently flavoured with allspice and oregano. The rich flavours of the lamb and sauce benefit from the contrasting fresh and simple tomato and radish salad, which was inspired by countless trips to the Eastern Med.

You may be thinking that potato mash doesn't exactly sound like an exotic accompaniment for such a traditional, spiced dish – and it isn't. It is, however, my dad's favourite starch and, I agree, sometimes it's the only thing in the world that will do. In this case, the delicious simple mash provides a bland creaminess that is the perfect vehicle to soak up all the yummy juices, so that nothing is wasted, and it goes surprisingly well with the spiciness of the roasted chops.

FOR THE MASH
750g/1lb 10oz new potatoes
30g/1oz butter
sea salt and freshly ground black
   pepper

FOR THE TARATOR SAUCE
1 slice of white bread
1 garlic clove
1 lemon
55g/2oz/heaped ⅓ cup pine nuts

1½ tsp ground cumin
55ml/1¾fl oz/scant ¼ cup olive oil

FOR THE LAMB CHOPS
8 small lamb chops (about
   90g/3¼oz each)
2 tsp ground allspice
2 tsp dried oregano
1 tbsp olive oil

FOR THE TOMATO AND RADISH
   SALAD
250g/9oz/heaped 1¾ cups cherry
   tomatoes
200g/7oz radishes
2 spring onions
1 handful of mint leaves
1 handful of parsley leaves
1 lemon
2 tbsp olive oil

PREHEAT THE OVEN to 200°C/400°F/Gas 6. To make the mash, cook the unpeeled potatoes in a large saucepan of boiling water for 15 minutes, or until tender. Drain, return them to the pan, then add the butter and a good pinch of salt and pepper. Mash together until fairly smooth, then cover and keep warm.

MEANWHILE, MAKE THE TARATOR SAUCE. Rip the bread into small pieces and put it into a food processor. Peel the garlic and add it to the food processor. Squeeze over the lemon juice and add the pine nuts, cumin and a good pinch of salt and pepper. Add 3 tablespoons water and the oil, then blend into a coarse sauce. Scoop the tarator sauce into a serving bowl, add a grinding of pepper, if you like, then cover and leave to one side.

LAY THE LAMB CHOPS on a chopping board and gently score both sides with a sharp knife. Put the lamb in a mixing bowl and add the allspice, oregano, oil and a good pinch of salt and pepper. Mix well so that the lamb is completely coated. Put the lamb on to a grill rack over a roasting tin and roast for 8–10 minutes until tender and juicy.

MAKE THE SALAD while the lamb cooks. Cut the cherry tomatoes and radishes in half and put them in a serving bowl. Trim and finely chop the spring onions with the mint leaves, if large, and add them, with the parsley leaves, to the tomatoes. Squeeze in the juice from the lemon, then pour over the oil and season with a good pinch of salt and pepper. Toss together well and leave to one side. Serve the cooked lamb and mash with the salad and tarator sauce.

Four Brothers Beef Curry SERVES **4** READY IN **30 MINUTES**

750g/1lb 10oz new potatoes
3 lemongrass stalks
3 garlic cloves
1 red chilli
2 tbsp groundnut oil
4 cardamom pods
2 star anise
5cm/2in cinnamon stick
4 cloves

400ml/14fl oz/generous 1½ cups
  coconut cream
2 tbsp tomato purée
2 tbsp fish sauce
1 tsp sugar
4 sirloin steaks (about 125g/4½oz
  each)
1 lime

CUT THE UNPEELED POTATOES in half, then cook them in a large saucepan of boiling water for 10–12 minutes until tender. Drain and leave in the colander.

MEANWHILE, **REMOVE THE TOUGH** outer leaves from the lemongrass and cut off the ends of the stalks. Peel the garlic and cut the top off the chilli. Chuck the lemongrass, garlic and chilli into a mini food processor, and blend into a paste.

HEAT THE OIL in a large, shallow saucepan over a medium heat and add the cardamom, star anise, cinnamon and cloves. Stir-fry for 30 seconds until fragrant, then tip in the spice paste and stir-fry for 10 seconds until it also releases its fragrance. Pour in the coconut cream and add the tomato purée, fish sauce and sugar. Mix everything together really well and simmer gently.

SLICE THE STEAKS into strips 5cm/2in wide and add them to the pan with the sauce. Carefully tip in the potatoes and mix well. Bring to the boil, then cover, reduce the heat to low and simmer gently for 5 minutes. Remove the lid and cook for another 10 minutes, stirring occasionally, until the beef is just cooked through and the sauce is brilliantly thick.

WHILE THE STEAK COOKS, cut the lime into quarters. Serve the curry with the wedges of lime to freshen it up.

SOUKS, SAND & BERBER BEEF STEW

Morocco is an enchanting country. I love all it has to offer, from the art and architecture to the people, dramatic landscapes and wonderful food. My research for *Mighty Spice Express* took me there for several weeks, which included eating my way around Fez, the fabulous coastal town of Essaouira and several trips to Marrakesh.

I spent a very happy day in the sunny capital wandering through the *medina*, avoiding the rug sellers and drinking lots of mint tea. I love a rooftop, and I found a good one with a postcard view of the city sprawled beneath the mighty Atlas Mountains, which were dusted with snow and gleaming under the vivid blue sky.

As the sun went down, the city came to life. The dusty souks were lit up by a thousand light bulbs, and hungry diners were lured out into the cool evening by the delicious smells that were cast into the air from the food stalls of the infamous Jamaa el-Fna square.

The stalls of Jamaa el-Fna sold everything. It was advanced street-food eating. I made several laps around the stalls and decided on a rich stew that was cooked in an earthenware pot called a *tangier*. The stew was simply made from meat, spices and butter, which had been left to cook for hours so that the flavour gods could work their magic and turn it into something sublime. All good things come to those who wait, but thankfully not in this book, because with a few clever changes I have recreated a rather special version of this sublime Berber beef stew that's ready in only 45 minutes. You must give it a go!

Berber Beef Stew SERVES **4** READY IN **45 MINUTES**

1 red onion
4 garlic cloves
1 carrot
2 courgettes
2 tbsp olive oil
600g/1lb 5oz beef fillet
2 tbsp tomato purée
2 tsp ground cumin

2 tsp ground ginger
1 tsp paprika
1 tsp freshly ground black pepper
½ tsp ground cinnamon
1 tsp flour
1 tbsp clear honey
150g/5½oz/heaped ¾ cup couscous
1 large handful of parsley leaves

1 preserved lemon
200g/7oz/heaped ¾ cup yogurt
2 tbsp harissa paste
2 tbsp toasted flaked almonds
sea salt

PEEL AND FINELY CHOP the onion and garlic, then peel the carrot. Chop the carrot and courgettes into 1cm/½in half-moons. Heat the oil in a large saucepan over a high heat and add the carrots and courgettes. Cook for 4 minutes, stirring frequently, to soften.

MEANWHILE, CUT THE BEEF into 2–3cm/¾–1¼in cubes and add to the cooked vegetables. Add the onion and garlic, and mix well. Reduce the heat to medium, add the tomato purée, cumin, ground ginger, paprika, black pepper, cinnamon, flour, honey and 250ml/9fl oz/1 cup boiling water. Mix well, bring to the boil, then cover and simmer for 10 minutes, or until the beef is just cooked through.

WHILE THE BEEF COOKS, put the couscous in a large mixing bowl and add 185ml/6fl oz/¾ cup warm water. Cover with cling film and leave for 10 minutes or until ready to eat.

FINELY CHOP THE PARSLEY while the couscous soaks. Remove the flesh from the preserved lemon and finely chop the skin. Leave to one side. Discard the flesh. Tip the yogurt into a serving bowl, then stir in the harissa, cover and leave to one side.

REMOVE THE LID from the cooked stew, turn the heat up to medium and cook for another 5 minutes, stirring occasionally, so that the sauce becomes lovely and thick. Throw the parsley and preserved lemon skin into the cooked stew, and mix well. Fluff up the couscous with a fork and divide into four bowls. Spoon over the stew, top with the almonds and serve with the harissa yogurt.

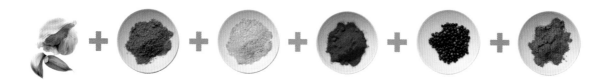

Mexican Sea Bream with Roasted Lemon Courgettes & Spicy Lime Seasoning SERVES **4** READY IN **40 MINUTES**

This meal tastes awesome and is so quick to make. The beauty of the dish comes from the flavour of the sauce, which has a pronounced smoky edge. I have taken a tip from Mexican cooking and charred the onion, garlic and tomatoes before chucking them into a blender with spices to make the sauce. This might sound a bit fussy, but it only takes a few extra minutes and it adds so much to the overall flavour – and the smokiness is exaggerated even more by using chipotle chillies. Cinnamon and paprika create a sweeter background note to the sauce, which works so well with the fish. The flavours marry together as the sauce gently cooks for a few minutes before the fish fillets are added.

The dish is completed with courgettes roasted until they become soft and melt into creaminess when you eat them, and the whole thing is fired up with a wicked little chilli, lime and salt seasoning to serve at the table.

FOR THE LEMON COURGETTES
600g/1lb 5oz courgettes
3 large thyme sprigs
2 tbsp olive oil
½ lemon
sea salt and freshly ground black
  pepper

**FOR THE SEA BREAM
  AND SAUCE**
2 chipotle chillies
1 red onion
4 garlic cloves
4 tomatoes
1 tsp ground cinnamon
½ tsp paprika
1 tsp brown sugar
leaves from 1 large thyme sprig
4 sea bream fillets (about
  125g/4½oz each)
1 handful of coriander leaves
2 tbsp best-quality extra virgin
  olive oil

**FOR THE SPICY LIME
  SEASONING**
2 limes
1 tsp crushed chilli flakes
1 tsp sea salt

TO SERVE
4 large flour tortillas

PREHEAT THE OVEN to 200°C/400°F/Gas 6. To make the lemon courgettes, cut the courgettes into 1.5cm/⅝in chunks and put them in a roasting tin. Add the thyme, olive oil and a good pinch of salt and pepper. Squeeze in the juice from the lemon and mix everything together well. Roast the courgettes for 30–35 minutes until tender and creamy.

MEANWHILE, SOAK THE CHIPOTLE CHILLIES for the sea bream sauce in 2 tablespoons hot water and leave to one side. Heat a non-stick frying pan over a high heat. While the pan heats, peel the onion and cut it into quarters, then peel the garlic. Carefully put them into the hot pan and toast for 2 minutes. Add the tomatoes and turn the garlic. Cook for another 2–3 minutes until the tomatoes and onion are charred on the cooked side and the garlic is charred on both sides.

WHILE THE TOMATOES ARE CHARRING, zest the limes for the spicy seasoning into a serving bowl and add the chilli flakes and salt. Leave to one side.

TRANSFER THE CHARRED INGREDIENTS and the chipotle chillies with their soaking liquid to a blender or food processor, and add the cinnamon, paprika, brown sugar, thyme and a good pinch of salt. Squeeze in the juice of 1½ of the limes used for the seasoning and blend into a smooth sauce.

POUR THE SAUCE into a large, shallow saucepan and bring to the boil over a medium heat. Cook for 10 minutes, stirring occasionally, then add the fish fillets, skin-side down, to the hot sauce. Cover and cook for 4–5 minutes until the fish is beautifully tender and flaky.

PINCH THE SPICY SEASONING mixture between your fingers to accentuate all the flavours while the fish cooks. Cut the remaining lime half into 4 segments.

SCATTER THE CORIANDER over the cooked fish and drizzle over the extra virgin olive oil. Serve the fish with the cooked courgettes, tortillas, lime segments and the spicy lime seasoning.

Dongbai Roast Cod with Stir-Fried Spinach & Peanuts SERVES **4** READY IN **25 MINUTES**

This meal is a nod to my time in Dongbai, China. Fish was always served as part of any meal, along with, frankly, everything – meat, shellfish, vegetables, soups, stews and dumplings. The tables groaned with food, and that's definitely one of my favourite sights. Preparing multiple dishes is hard work, so I have stripped things back for this simple but mouth-watering version.

The combination of chilli flakes, sesame seeds and cumin seeds was my favourite discovery from this region of Northern China. The three flavours work perfectly together. I grind one-half of the mix to a powder and leave the rest whole to create a spicy coating for the fish that has a crunchy texture. The spices are enhanced by the rich flavours of oyster sauce, soy sauce and honey, giving the coating a salty–sweet base. These are big flavours, and the cod loves them all.

The simple spinach and peanut stir-fry is slightly tart to complement the sticky roast cod. Traditionally, this would be made with Chinese black vinegar, but this is hard to find and I actually really like the flavour of red wine vinegar and soy sauce used here instead.

FOR THE RICE
250g/9oz/1¼ cups jasmine rice

FOR THE ROAST COD
2 tsp crushed chilli flakes
2 tbsp sesame seeds
2 tsp cumin seeds

6 tbsp oyster sauce
2 tbsp soy sauce
1 tbsp clear honey
1½ tbsp groundnut oil
4 skinless cod fillets (about
　175g/6oz each)

FOR THE SPINACH AND
　PEANUTS
1 tbsp chilli oil
55g/2oz/heaped ⅓ cup peanuts
400g/14oz spinach
1 tbsp light soy sauce
2 tsp red wine vinegar

PREHEAT THE OVEN to 200°C/400°F/Gas 6. Cook the rice in boiling water for 10–12 minutes until soft, or as directed on the packet, then drain in a colander. Pour boiling water into the saucepan to a depth of 2.5cm/1in and heat over a low heat. Put the colander with the rice over the pan and leave to steam gently until you are ready to eat.

MEANWHILE, PUT HALF THE CHILLI FLAKES, sesame seeds and cumin seeds for the roast cod into a spice grinder and grind into a fine powder. Tip into a mixing bowl and add the oyster sauce, soy sauce, honey and 1 tablespoon of the oil, and mix well. Add the fish and mix well so that the fillets are completely coated.

LAY THE FISH in a small roasting tin in a single layer and spoon the remaining marinade over the top. Sprinkle most of the remaining chilli flakes, sesame seeds and cumin seeds over the top, and drizzle over the remaining oil. Roast for 12–15 minutes until the fish is cooked through, tender and flaky.

MAKE THE SPINACH AND PEANUTS while the fish cooks. Heat a wok over a high heat and add the chilli oil and peanuts. Stir-fry for 1 minute, or until just turning golden. Add the spinach and continue to stir-fry for 2–3 minutes until wilted. Drain off the excess moisture and return the wok to a high heat. Pour in the soy sauce and red wine vinegar, and continue to stir-fry for another 1 minute. Sprinkle over the remaining chilli flakes, sesame seeds and cumin seeds. Serve the fish with the sticky rice and the spinach. Remember to spoon over all the lovely juices from the roasting tin, as they are too good to waste.

Prawn & Herb Brewat
with Vermicelli Rice Noodles SERVES **4** READY IN **30 MINUTES**

FOR THE PRAWN AND HERB BREWAT
1 red onion
4 garlic cloves
2 tbsp olive oil
200g/7oz/heaped 1⅓ cups cherry tomatoes
250g/9oz/1 cup tomato passata
1 tsp clear honey
2 tsp ground cumin
1 tsp paprika

½ tsp chilli powder
½ tsp freshly ground black pepper
½ lemon
100ml/3½fl oz/generous ⅓ cup vegetable stock
1 large handful of coriander leaves and stalks
500g/1lb 2oz raw, peeled king prawns (with or without tails)

FOR THE RICE NOODLES
1 large handful of coriander leaves
200g/7oz vermicelli rice noodles
2 tbsp olive oil
½ tsp ground cumin
¼ tsp chilli powder
½ lemon
sea salt and freshly ground black pepper

PEEL AND FINELY CHOP the onion and garlic. Heat the oil in a large saucepan over a medium heat. Add the onion and garlic and stir-fry for 4–5 minutes until golden.

MEANWHILE, CUT THE CHERRY TOMATOES in half, then add them to the cooked onion. Add the passata, honey, cumin, paprika, chilli powder, black pepper and a good pinch of salt. Squeeze in the juice from the lemon and add the stock. Mix everything together really well, then bring to the boil. Cover and reduce the heat to low. Cook for 10 minutes, stirring occasionally, to allow the sauce to develop in flavour.

ROUGHLY CHOP THE CORIANDER for both the brewat and the noodles, and keep in separate piles. When the sauce has cooked, turn the heat up to medium and add the prawns and the pile of chopped coriander leaves and stalks. Cook for 5–6 minutes, stirring occasionally, until the prawns have cooked through and turned pink.

WHILE THE PRAWNS COOK, cook the noodles in boiling water for 2–3 minutes until soft, or as directed on the packet. Drain and return them to the pan. Add the oil, the chopped coriander leaves, the cumin, chilli powder and a good pinch of salt and pepper. Squeeze in the juice from the lemon and mix everything together well so that all the spices and dressing completely coat the yummy noodles. Serve with the cooked prawn and herb brewat.

Rita's Tamarind & Coconut Prawn Curry SERVES **4** READY IN **20 MINUTES**

This is a super-quick prawn curry, which is hot, sweet and sour all at once. If you can't find tamarind, just squeeze in the juice of a lime. And chilli powder and freshly ground black pepper are fine if you don't have the whole spices.

250g/9oz/1¼ cups basmati rice
2 onions
2 tbsp groundnut oil
3 dried red chillies
10 peppercorns

1 tsp paprika
½ tsp turmeric
400ml/14fl oz/generous 1½ cups
  coconut milk
3 tsp tamarind paste

500g/1lb 2oz raw, peeled king
  prawns (with or without tails)
1 handful of coriander leaves
sea salt

COOK THE RICE in boiling water for 10–12 minutes until soft, or as directed on the packet. Drain in a colander and return to the pan. Cover the pan with a clean tea towel and then the lid. Leave to one side so that the rice can fluff up ready to eat.

MEANWHILE, PEEL AND FINELY SLICE the onions. Heat the oil in a large saucepan over a medium heat and add the onions. Cook for 4–5 minutes, stirring occasionally, or until just turning golden.

WHILE THE ONIONS COOK, chuck the chillies and peppercorns into a spice grinder, and grind into a fine powder. Tip the ground spices into the pan with the cooked onions and add the paprika, turmeric and a good pinch of salt.

MIX WELL, pour in the coconut milk and add the tamarind paste. Mix everything together really well so that the sauce takes on a rich red colour. Bring to the boil and add the prawns. Give them a good stir in the hot sauce, then cover and cook for 5–6 minutes, stirring occasionally, until the prawns are cooked through and beautifully pink. Meanwhile, roughly chop the coriander. Scatter the coriander over the cooked curry and serve with the rice.

Condesa Smoky Beans with Green Salsa SERVES **4** READY IN **30 MINUTES**

FOR THE RICE
250g/9oz/1¼ cups long grain rice

FOR THE SMOKY BEANS
1 chipotle chilli
800g/1lb 12oz/4 cups tinned pinto beans
1 red pepper
1 red onion
2 tbsp olive oil
2 bay leaves

4 garlic cloves
1 tsp ground cinnamon
2 tsp ground cumin
400g/14oz/scant 1⅔ cups tinned chopped tomatoes
1½ tbsp clear honey
55g/2oz Gruyère cheese
sea salt

FOR THE GREEN SALSA
1 avocado
3 spring onions
1 green chilli
2 large handfuls of coriander leaves and stalks
2 tbsp olive oil
1 lime

COOK THE RICE in boiling water for 10–12 minutes until soft, or as directed on the packet. Drain in a colander, then cover the rice with a clean tea towel while still in the colander and leave to one side. Meanwhile, cut the chipotle chilli for the beans in half and put both halves in a small bowl. Cover with 2–3 tablespoons boiling water and leave to one side to soften for a couple of minutes.

DRAIN AND RINSE THE BEANS and leave to one side. Deseed the pepper and peel the onion, then finely chop both. Heat the oil in a large saucepan over a high heat and add the pepper and onion. Stir-fry for 3 minutes to soften, then reduce the heat to medium and add the bay leaves. Peel and crush in the garlic. Mix well.

ADD THE CINNAMON, cumin, tomatoes, honey and beans to the onion mixture. Season with salt. Pour in the chipotle and its water. Mix well, then cover and cook for 15 minutes, stirring occasionally, or until the beans are hot and the sauce is thick.

MAKE THE GREEN SALSA. Cut the avocado in half and remove the stone with a knife. Scoop out the flesh into a blender or food processor. Trim the spring onions and discard the top of the chilli, then chuck them into the blender with the coriander, oil and some salt. Squeeze in the lime and blend into a coarse salsa. Tip into a serving bowl. Serve the rice and beans with the cheese grated over the top and with the salsa.

Amish's Gujarati Vegetable Curry SERVES **4** READY IN **35 MINUTES**

This magnificent curry can be made well in advance. Simply make the sauce and cook it without adding any of the vegetables. Cook the vegetables, then refresh them under cold water. When you want to eat, reheat the sauce and add the vegetables. Cook until the veg have warmed through, then serve.

250g/9oz/1¼ cups basmati rice
400g/14oz/scant 2 cups tinned
  chickpeas
1 onion
2 tbsp groundnut oil
2.5cm/1in piece fresh root ginger
6 garlic cloves

4 tomatoes
85g/3oz/heaped ½ cup
  cashew nuts
2 tsp ground coriander
1 tsp ground cumin
1 tsp garam masala
½ tsp chilli powder

½ tsp turmeric
400g/14oz new potatoes
3 carrots
1 small cauliflower
200g/7oz green beans
1 handful of coriander leaves
sea salt

COOK THE RICE in boiling water for 10–12 minutes until soft, or as directed on the packet. Drain and rinse the chickpeas in a colander. In the same colander, drain the rice then tip the rice and chickpeas back into the pan. Cover the pan with a clean tea towel and then the lid. Leave to one side so that the rice can fluff up ready to eat.

MEANWHILE, PEEL AND FINELY CHOP the onion. Heat the oil in a large saucepan over a medium heat and add the onion. Cook for 4–5 minutes, stirring occasionally, until golden.

PEEL THE GINGER and garlic, then chuck both into a blender or food processor with the tomatoes, 55g/2oz/heaped ⅓ cup of the cashew nuts, the ground coriander, cumin, garam masala, chilli powder, turmeric and a good pinch of salt. Blend until smooth. Pour this mixture over the cooked onion, mix well and bring to the boil. Cover, reduce the heat to low and simmer for 20 minutes, stirring occasionally.

CUT THE POTATOES into quarters while the sauce cooks. Cook them in a saucepan of boiling water for 8 minutes. Peel the carrots, then cut them, with the cauliflower, into small pieces. Cut the beans in half. Add the vegetables to the potatoes and cook for 5–6 minutes until tender, then drain. Roughly chop the coriander. Mix the vegetables into the sauce. Serve the curry and rice, sprinkled with coriander and cashew nuts.

Beirut Ratatouille SERVES **4**   READY IN **45 MINUTES**

1 red onion
4 garlic cloves
2 tbsp olive oil
150g/5½oz button mushrooms
2 red peppers
1 aubergine
1 courgette
400g/14oz/scant 2 cups tinned
  chickpeas
55g/2oz/scant ¼ cup tomato purée
400g/14oz/scant 1⅔ cups tinned
  chopped tomatoes

3 tsp ground cumin
2 tsp paprika
½ tsp chilli powder
½ tsp freshly ground black pepper
1 large handful of parsley leaves
sea salt

TO SERVE
1 lemon
1 bag of mixed salad leaves

PEEL AND FINELY CHOP the onion and garlic. Heat the oil in a large saucepan over a medium heat and add the onion and garlic, and mix well. Roughly slice the mushrooms, then add them to the pan with the onion. Mix everything together and cook for 3–4 minutes, stirring occasionally, until the mushrooms have cooked down.

MEANWHILE, DESEED THE PEPPERS, then, chop the peppers, aubergine and courgette into 2cm/¾in cubes. Drain and rinse the chickpeas. Transfer the vegetables to the pan with the cooked mushrooms and add the chickpeas, tomato purée, tinned tomatoes, cumin, paprika, chilli powder, black pepper and a really good pinch of salt.

POUR IN 320ml/11fl oz/scant 1⅓ cups boiling water and mix well. Increase the heat to high and bring to the boil. Cover, leaving a slight gap to allow the excess steam to escape, then reduce the heat to medium and simmer for 25–30 minutes, stirring occasionally, until the vegetables are cooked through but still have a little bite.

AS THE RATATOUILLE SIMMERS, finely chop the parsley and cut the lemon into wedges. Tip the salad into a serving bowl. Just before serving, mix the chopped parsley into the ratatouille. Serve with the lemon wedges and the mixed salad.

SOMETHING SPECTACULAR

There are times when you want to pull out all the stops, get out the fancy tableware, polish the glasses you've been saving for the Queen and cook something unbelievable. In this chapter the recipes use fabulous ingredients to create spectacular dinners that can all be made super-quick – and none in more than 45 minutes. My Beautiful Beef Mezze – roasted fillet of beef, coated in spices and served with a spinach *raita*, and a tangy red onion and herb salad – takes only 40 minutes to make. Or my delicious Kashmiri Lamb Cutlets, served with a vibrant Pineapple & Chilli Salad & Mint & Lime Raita, is utterly mind-blowing and ready for the table in 30 minutes. My delicate Essaouira Monkfish Tagine, flavoured with preserved lemon, cumin, paprika and garlic, takes only 30 minutes to make, so even if you don't have much time you can still impress your guests with something spectacular.

Chicken with Mexican Chilli-Chocolate Mole, Polenta & Fennel Salad SERVES **4** READY IN **45 MINUTES**

Mole is an exquisite Mexican sauce with a complex flavour. It requires lots of ingredients and time, but I have created an express version that has all the depth of flavour of a traditional *mole*, without the fuss. Bright yellow polenta is just right to soak up all the intense flavours and is reminiscent of the corn used in Mexican cooking. My fennel salad, with crunchy radishes and a tart dressing, adds vibrancy and balances the flavours of the dish.

FOR THE CHILLI-CHOCOLATE MOLE
6 garlic cloves
55g/2oz/heaped ⅓ cup peanuts
4 cloves
2 chipotle chillies
1 onion
3 tbsp olive oil
400g/14oz/scant 1⅔ cups tinned chopped tomatoes
1 tsp ground cinnamon
1½ tsp ground cumin
2 tsp dried oregano
2 tsp brown sugar
30g/1oz dark chocolate (70–85% cocoa solids)

FOR THE FENNEL SALAD
100g/3½oz radishes
2 fennel bulbs
½ lime
2 tbsp olive oil
sea salt and freshly ground black pepper

FOR THE GRIDDLED CHICKEN
2 tbsp olive oil
4 skinless chicken breasts
1 tbsp sesame seeds

FOR THE POLENTA
200g/7oz/1⅓ cups quick-cook polenta
25g/1oz butter

FIRST, MAKE THE MOLE. Heat a large frying pan over a medium heat, then peel the garlic and add it to the pan with the peanuts and cloves. Toast for 4–5 minutes, shaking the pan occasionally, until the peanuts have started turning golden. While they toast, put the chillies in a bowl and pour over 2 tablespoons boiling water to soften them. Peel the onion and cut it into quarters.

PUT THE TOASTED PEANUTS, cloves and garlic into a blender or food processor. Tip in the chillies and their soaking water and add the onion, oil, tomatoes, cinnamon, cumin, oregano, brown sugar and a really good pinch of salt. Blend for 2 minutes so that the sauce becomes beautifully smooth. Pour the sauce into a saucepan and bring to the boil over a medium heat. Cover, reduce the heat to low and simmer for 20 minutes.

MEANWHILE, MAKE THE SALAD. Cut the radishes into quarters and put them in a serving bowl. Shave the fennel using a slicer or mandolin and add to the bowl with the radish. Squeeze over the juice from the lime, pour in the oil and season with salt and pepper. Mix everything together really well, then cover and leave to one side.

TO MAKE THE GRIDDLED CHICKEN, heat a griddle until smoking and rub the olive oil all over the chicken breasts. Griddle for 10–12 minutes on each side until cooked through and tender. Remove the pan from the heat and leave to one side.

WHEN THE MOLE SAUCE HAS SIMMERED for 20 minutes, break in the chocolate and mix well. Cook for another 10 minutes, stirring occasionally, so that the flavours develop even more.

MAKE THE POLENTA while the sauce finishes cooking. Pour the polenta into a saucepan and whisk in 800ml/28fl oz/scant 3½ cups boiling water. Cook over a low heat for 1–2 minutes, stirring continuously, until the water is absorbed and the polenta cooked. Stir in the butter and a good pinch of salt and pepper. Serve the polenta with the chicken, and pour the rich, velvety brown mole sauce over the top. Sprinkle each serving with sesame seeds and serve with the salad.

Saffron Chicken Mansaf with Tahini Yogurt & Green Salad SERVES **4** READY IN **40 MINUTES**

A *mansaf* is a Jordanian dish traditionally made with lamb and served on a huge platter. The lamb is cooked with a thick yogurt sauce and served on a bed of rice, with nuts and herbs scattered over the top. It's a dish meant for sharing, as is this fast interpretation.

My version is made with chicken thighs instead of lamb and is seriously spiced up with saffron, cinnamon, cardamom and a heavy grating of nutmeg. Instead of making a traditional yogurt sauce, I have included a speedy variation using yogurt blended with wonderfully rich tahini and a squeeze of fresh lemon juice. Although I have used parsley, pine nuts and almonds to serve with the *mansaf*, you could add other herbs and nuts instead. Go crazy – for a great *mansaf*, the more you throw on top the better! The only thing I would insist on is that you share your *mansaf* with friends and family over a really good bottle of wine!

FOR THE SAFFRON CHICKEN MANSAF
350g/12oz/1¾ cups basmati rice
600ml/21fl oz/scant 2½ cups chicken stock
¼ tsp saffron threads
2 onions
3 tbsp olive oil
6 cardamom pods
4 garlic cloves
2 tsp ground cinnamon

3 bay leaves
500g/1lb 2oz boneless, skinless chicken thighs
55g/2oz/heaped ⅓ cup pine nuts
1 large handful of parsley leaves
½ nutmeg
55g/2oz/scant ⅔ cup flaked almonds
sea salt and freshly ground black pepper

FOR THE TAHINI YOGURT
300g/10½oz/scant 1¼ cups yogurt
2 tbsp tahini
½ lemon

TO SERVE
1 bag of green salad

PUT THE RICE in a bowl, cover with cold water and stir. Leave to one side for a few minutes to soak and allow the starch to release. Pour the stock into a saucepan and bring to the boil over a medium heat. Once boiled, add the saffron, stir well and remove from the heat.

MEANWHILE, PEEL AND SLICE THE ONIONS. Heat the oil in a large, shallow saucepan over a medium heat and add the onions. Mix well and cook for 4–5 minutes, stirring occasionally, until golden.

CRUSH THE CARDAMOM PODS by pressing down with the side of a knife, and add them to the cooked onions. Peel and crush in the garlic, then add the cinnamon, bay leaves and a good pinch of salt. Drain the rice and tip it into the pan. Mix well so that the grains become coated in the oil and spices. Pour over the saffron stock and stir gently. Put the chicken thighs on the top of the rice and poke them down with a spoon. Bring to the boil, cover, reduce the heat to low and cook for 20 minutes, or until the chicken is cooked through and the rice is tender.

WHILE THE CHICKEN AND RICE COOK, put the pine nuts in a small frying pan over a medium heat and toast for 4–5 minutes, shaking the pan occasionally, until golden. Remove from the heat and leave to one side.

TO MAKE THE TAHINI YOGURT, tip the yogurt into a serving bowl, add the tahini and a good pinch of salt. Squeeze in the juice from the lemon, mix well and add a grinding of pepper. Leave to one side.

FINELY CHOP THE PARSLEY and leave to one side, then tip the salad into a serving bowl. Once the saffron mansaf is cooked, grate over the nutmeg and add half the pine nuts, flaked almonds and parsley. Season with salt and pepper, and mix well with a fork. Scatter over the remaining nuts and parsley, and serve with the yogurt and green salad.

COOL CHILLIES, TEQUILA & TOSTADAS

The beautiful city of Oaxaca, in southern Mexico, has a really cool arty vibe. Little galleries are scattered throughout the city and the whole place is painted a veritable array of different colours. Art, music, dance and food form the cornerstone of life in Oaxaca, and it provided a fantastic backdrop for my quest to find the best *tostadas*. *Tostadas* are the crunchy backbone of Mexican food – a crispy corn tortilla base covered in delicious toppings. It makes the perfect on-the-go street food.

I went high end with beautifully grilled octopus *tostadas* served on a fancy slate board and ate shredded pork *tostadas* with avocado and chilli from a food cart. I also hit on Mercado Benito Juárez, a huge indoor market that was filled with wonderful fresh produce and awesome street food. They had deep-fried grasshoppers covered in salt and chilli (the Mexican equivalent of crunchy chilli peanuts to have with cheeky *cerveza*), spicy broths flavoured with coriander and lime, black beans served with soft tortillas for dunking and ginormous *tostadas*. The *tostadas* were actually more like pizzas – a crispy base slathered in refried beans and topped with the famous Oaxaca *queso* (cheese).

I have combined elements from all my favourite *tostadas* to create a really fancy street-food-inspired dinner, Duck Tostadas with Black Beans & Salsa. It's a thing of deliciousness and takes only 35 minutes to make! Oh yeah, and add a shot of gold tequila before you eat, and you have a party.

Duck Tostadas with Black Beans & Salsa SERVES **4** READY IN **35 MINUTES**

FOR THE ROAST DUCK
4 duck breasts (about 150g/5½oz each)
4 garlic cloves
2 tsp smoked paprika
½ tsp chilli powder
2 tbsp olive oil

FOR THE BLACK BEANS
400g/14oz/2 cups tinned black beans
2 tbsp olive oil
1½ tsp ground cumin
½ lime
sea salt and freshly ground black pepper

FOR THE SALSA
1 red onion
115g/4oz/heaped ¾ cup drained sun-dried tomatoes in oil
1 tsp smoked paprika
½ lime

TO SERVE
1 lettuce
2 large handfuls of coriander leaves
4 large tortillas

PREHEAT THE OVEN to 200°C/400°F/Gas 6. Trim and score the skin on the duck breasts, and put them in a small roasting tin. Peel and crush over the garlic, and add the smoked paprika, chilli powder, oil and a good pinch of salt. Mix well so that the duck is completely coated. Turn the duck skin-side up, then roast for 25–30 minutes until golden on the outside and juicy and pink in the centre.

MEANWHILE, DRAIN AND RINSE the beans and tip them into a saucepan over a medium heat. Mash the beans, using a potato masher, until fairly smooth, then add 55ml/1¾fl oz/scant ¼ cup water, the olive oil and cumin. Squeeze in the juice from the lime, season with salt and pepper, and mix well. Bring to the boil, reduce the heat to low and cook for 8–10 minutes, stirring occasionally, until warmed through and thick. Remove from the heat, cover and leave to one side.

TO MAKE THE SALSA, peel the onion and cut it into quarters, then chuck it into a food processor, and add the sun-dried tomatoes, smoked paprika and a pinch of salt. Squeeze in the juice from the lime, blend until smooth, then pour into a serving bowl.

FINELY SLICE the lettuce and coriander, then put them on to a serving plate. Put the tortillas on four serving plates and cover each one with the beans. Slice up the duck and put on top of the beans. Serve with the salad and salsa.

Paprika & Fennel Pork Chops with Lentils & Beetroot & Goat's Cheese Salad SERVES **4** READY IN **30 MINUTES**

All my favourite flavours are brought together in this meal – pork, paprika, fennel, garlic, chorizo, lentils, beetroot and goat's cheese. Although there's a lot going on, these big flavours go together splendidly and cook super-quickly. Fennel seeds and smoked paprika make an aromatic crust for pork chops that are grilled to perfection. Chorizo fried with garlic, plus my favourite sun-dried tomato paste, enrich the lentils. And, finally, a quick salad of rocket, goat's cheese and beetroot adds colour, lightness and a little crunch to the meal. All this in 30 minutes – now that really *is* something spectacular!

FOR THE SPICED PORK CHOPS
1 tbsp fennel seeds
2 tsp smoked paprika
4 pork chops (about 200g/7oz each)
2 tbsp olive oil

FOR THE LENTILS
115g/4oz chorizo, in one piece
2 garlic cloves
1 tbsp olive oil
400g/14oz/1½ cups tinned green lentils
2 tbsp sun-dried tomato paste
1 handful of parsley leaves
sea salt and freshly ground black pepper

FOR THE BEETROOT AND GOAT'S CHEESE SALAD
200g/7oz cooked, peeled beetroot
½ orange
1 tbsp olive oil
1 handful of rocket leaves
55g/2oz soft goat's cheese
¼ red chilli

PREHEAT THE GRILL to high. Lightly crush the fennel seeds using a mortar and pestle or a spice grinder. Tip them into a mixing bowl and add the paprika and a good pinch of salt. Put the pork into a separate mixing bowl and pour over the olive oil. Mix well.

TRANSFER THE PORK to a grill rack and rub the spice mix over the top of the chops to completely coat them in a crust of fantastic spice. Grill the chops for 6–8 minutes on each side until golden and cooked through.

WHILE THE PORK COOKS, finely chop the chorizo for the lentils and peel and chop the garlic. Heat the oil in a frying pan over a medium heat and add the chorizo and garlic. Cook for 3–4 minutes, stirring occasionally, until the chorizo turns golden. Drain and rinse the lentils, then tip them into the pan with the cooked chorizo. Add the sun-dried tomato paste, 125ml/4fl oz/½ cup boiling water and season with a pinch of salt and pepper. Mix well, reduce the heat to low and simmer gently, stirring occasionally, while you make the salad.

TIP THE BEETROOT into a mixing bowl and cut into small pieces using a knife and fork (this helps to avoid pink hands and chopping board). Squeeze over the juice from the orange, pour in the oil and add a pinch of salt and pepper. Mix well and tip out on to a serving plate. Scatter the rocket over the beetroot and crumble the goat's cheese over the top. Deseed and finely chop the chilli, then sprinkle it over the salad. Cover and leave to one side.

FINELY CHOP THE PARSLEY for the lentils and add it to the pan with the warmed lentils. Turn the heat up to high, mix well and cook for 1–2 minutes, stirring continuously, until thick. Serve the pork chops, spice-side up, with the lentils and the salad at the table.

Lao Lap Aubergines & Pork SERVES **4** READY IN **30 MINUTES**

2 red chillies
6 garlic cloves
5 tbsp groundnut oil
2 aubergines
2 tbsp fish sauce

3 tbsp dark soy sauce
250g/9oz/1¼ cups jasmine rice
2 lemongrass stalks
1 handful of dill
1 handful of coriander leaves

1 handful of mint leaves
500g/1lb 2oz minced pork
1 lime
1 handful of bean sprouts

CUT THE TOP OFF 1 of the chillies, then slice the chilli. Peel the garlic, then slice 3 of the garlic cloves. Heat 3 tablespoons of the oil in a large frying pan over a medium-low heat and add the sliced chilli and garlic. Mix well and cook, stirring occasionally, while you prepare the aubergines.

SLICE THE AUBERGINES into 5mm/¼in discs and layer them in the pan. Pour over 1 tablespoon of the fish sauce and 2 tablespoons water. Cover and cook for 20 minutes, or until tender, shaking the pan occasionally and turning the aubergines halfway through cooking. Remove the lid and pour in 2 tablespoons of the soy sauce. Turn the heat up to medium and cook for 4–5 minutes, shaking the pan occasionally, until the aubergines have taken on a little colour.

MEANWHILE, COOK THE RICE in boiling water for 10–12 minutes until soft, or as directed on the packet, then drain in a colander. While the rice cooks, remove the tough outer leaves from the lemongrass and cut off the ends of the stalks. Cut the top off the remaining chilli. Put the lemongrass, chilli and remaining garlic into a mini food processor. Blend into a rough paste. Finely chop half the herbs and leave to one side.

HEAT A WOK over a high heat until smoking. Add the remaining oil and the pork. Stir-fry for 2 minutes, then add the spice paste and stir-fry for another 2–3 minutes until the pork is just cooked through. Add the remaining fish sauce and soy sauce. Squeeze in the juice from the lime and stir-fry for 1 minute. Turn off the heat, chuck in the chopped herbs, mix well and leave to one side. Put the cooked aubergines on a large serving plate, spoon over the pork and top with the remaining herbs and the bean sprouts. Serve with the rice.

Kashmiri Lamb Cutlets with Pineapple & Chilli Salad & Mint & Lime Raita SERVES **4** READY IN **30 MINUTES**

These lamb cutlets are flavoured with wonderfully mild and beautifully red Kashmiri chillies, plus the warmth of ginger, cloves and garlic. The final grating of creamed coconut over the lamb adds a hint of richness as it melts through. The flavour of the Kashmiri chillies is unmistakable and makes biting into the charred lamb a joyous experience. With every meal I eat I like to have a balance of flavours and textures, and the lamb screams out for something fresh and juicy. My salad of pineapple, chilli, tomatoes, olives, mint and lime freshens things up in a blast of colour and flavour, and the whole dish is finished off nicely with a mint and lime *raita*.

FOR THE LAMB CUTLETS
4 dried Kashmiri chillies
8 cloves
10 black peppercorns
2.5cm/1in cinnamon stick
1 tsp sea salt
1 tsp sugar
2.5cm/1in piece fresh root ginger
4 garlic cloves
2 tbsp white wine vinegar
2 tbsp olive oil
8 lamb cutlets
25g/1oz creamed coconut

TO SERVE
4 flatbreads

**FOR THE PINEAPPLE AND
    CHILLI SALAD**
1 red chilli
½ pineapple
150g/5½oz/1 cup cherry tomatoes
1 carrot
100g/3½oz/heaped 1 cup bean
    sprouts
30g/1oz/¼ cup pitted black olives
1 handful of mint leaves
1 lime
2 tbsp olive oil
sea salt

FOR THE MINT AND LIME RAITA
250g/9oz/1 cup yogurt
½ lime
1 handful of mint leaves
1 tbsp olive oil
a pinch of chilli powder

PREHEAT THE GRILL to high and the oven to 180°C/350°F/Gas 4. Put the Kashmiri chillies, cloves, peppercorns, cinnamon, salt and sugar in a spice grinder, and grind to a powder. Peel and add the ginger and garlic with the white wine vinegar and oil, then blend into a smooth paste.

PUT THE LAMB CUTLETS in a mixing bowl and tip in the spice paste. Mix everything together really well so that all the lamb is completely coated. Put the lamb on to a grill rack and grill for 6–8 minutes on each side until golden on the outside and pink and juicy in the centre.

WHILE THE LAMB COOKS, pop the flatbreads into the hot oven and turn it off, so that they warm through and don't burn. Next, make the salad. Cut the top off the chilli and roll the chilli between your hands to deseed it, then chop it finely and chuck it in a large mixing bowl. Cut the top and bottom off the pineapple, then stand it upright on your chopping board. Slice off the skin, cutting downwards from top to bottom. Carefully cut out any pieces of skin left on the fruit. Cut the pineapple half in half lengthways, then slice off the woody core so that you are left with the soft flesh.

CHOP THE PINEAPPLE FLESH into small chunks and cut the cherry tomatoes in half. Add them to the bowl with the chilli. Peel and then coarsely grate the carrot into the bowl, and add the bean sprouts and olives. Chop the mint leaves, if large, and chuck them in the bowl with the salad. Squeeze in the juice from the lime, pour over the oil and season with salt. Mix everything together really well.

TO MAKE THE RAITA, tip the yogurt into a serving bowl, squeeze in the juice from the lime and season with a pinch of salt. Finely chop the mint and add it to the bowl. Mix well, drizzle with the oil and top with a pinch of chilli powder. Serve the cooked lamb with the creamed coconut grated over the top and the vibrant salad, raita and warm flatbreads at the table.

Manchurian Lamb with Tamarind Slaw & Griddled Chilli Potatoes SERVES **4** READY IN **40 MINUTES**

FOR THE ROAST LAMB
1 tsp Sichuan pepper
2 tbsp sesame seeds
2 tsp cumin seeds
600g/1lb 5oz trimmed neck or
  loin lamb fillet
2 tbsp olive oil
sea salt

FOR THE GRIDDLED POTATOES
500g/1lb 2oz new potatoes
2 tbsp chilli oil

FOR THE TAMARIND SLAW
2 tbsp tamarind paste
3 tsp clear honey
2 tsp soy sauce

2 tsp sesame oil
450g/1lb white cabbage
4 spring onions
½ red chilli
1 handful of coriander leaves

PREHEAT THE OVEN to 200°C/400°F/Gas 6. Put half the Sichuan pepper, sesame seeds and cumin seeds into a spice grinder and grind until smooth. Tip into a serving bowl and add the remaining spices and a good pinch of salt. Mix together really well.

IF USING LOIN FILLET, pull off the membrane. Cut the lamb into 7.5–10cm/3–4in pieces and put in a small roasting tin. Pour over the olive oil and mix well. Sprinkle over two-thirds of the mixed spices and rub all over the lamb. Roast for 15–20 minutes until cooked through and really tender.

MEANWHILE, BOIL THE POTATOES for 12–15 minutes until tender. While the lamb and potatoes cook, make the slaw. Mix the tamarind paste, honey, soy sauce, sesame oil and 2 tablespoons water in a mixing bowl. Grate the cabbage using the fine setting of a food processor, then tip into the bowl with the dressing. Trim and finely slice the spring onions, then finely chop the chilli and coriander. Chuck them into the bowl with the cabbage and toss together. Tip into a serving bowl, then cover.

HEAT A GRIDDLE over a high heat. Meanwhile, drain the cooked potatoes and return them to the pan. Pour in the chilli oil and add a pinch of the mixed spices and a small pinch of salt. Mix well, and don't be afraid to break up a few of the potatoes. Tip the potatoes on to the hot griddle and cook for 2 minutes on each side, or until they start to crisp up, shaking the pan occasionally. Slice the lamb and sprinkle a little of the spices over the top. Serve with the potatoes and slaw, with the remaining spices at the table.

Sticky Malaysian Lamb with Penang Garden Rice
SERVES **4**   READY IN **40 MINUTES**

FOR THE STICKY LAMB
4 lamb rump steaks (about
  150g/5½oz each)
1 tsp Chinese five-spice powder
2 tbsp rice wine
2 tbsp oyster sauce
1 tbsp light soy sauce
1 tsp sesame oil

1 tsp olive oil

FOR THE PENANG RICE
350g/12oz/1¾ cups basmati rice
2.5cm/1in piece fresh root ginger
1 onion
2 lemongrass stalks
2 tbsp groundnut oil

1 tsp fenugreek seeds
2.5cm/1in cinnamon stick
4 cardamom pods
3 star anise
400ml/14fl oz/generous 1½ cups
  coconut milk
1 small handful of coriander leaves
3 tbsp fish sauce

PREHEAT THE OVEN to 200°C/400°F/Gas 6. Put the lamb in a small roasting tin and add the Chinese five-spice powder, rice wine, oyster sauce, soy sauce, sesame oil and olive oil. Mix well and leave to one side to marinate.

PUT THE RICE in a large saucepan, cover with cold water and stir, and then leave to one side for 5 minutes to soak.

PEEL THE GINGER and onion, then finely chop both. Bash the fat ends of the lemongrass with a wooden spoon. Heat the groundnut oil in a shallow saucepan over a medium heat and add the fenugreek, cinnamon, cardamom and star anise. Stir-fry for 30 seconds until fragrant, then add the onion and ginger. Cook for 4–5 minutes, stirring occasionally, until the onion has started to turn golden.

MEANWHILE, POP THE LAMB into the oven for 15–20 minutes until cooked through and tender.

TIP THE SOAKED RICE into a colander, then add it to the pan with the cooked onion and spices. Pour over 400ml/14fl oz/generous 1½ cups hot water and the coconut milk. Pop the lemongrass in the pan, then stir and cover. Reduce the heat to low and simmer gently for 10–15 minutes until all the water has been absorbed and the rice is tender. You can always add extra hot water if the rice needs it. Slice the cooked lamb.

CHOP THE CORIANDER, then season the cooked rice with the fish sauce. Tip into a serving dish. Serve the lamb on the rice, sprinkled with coriander.

Beautiful Beef Mezze SERVES **4** READY IN **40 MINUTES**

I always enjoy a mezze – a table laden with wonderful home-made food to pass around to great friends and family, while the conversation and wine flow. I couldn't resist including a super-fast version in this book, and this beef mezze, inspired by the Eastern Mediterranean, has it all – spice-encrusted roast beef, a spinach *raita*, a crunchy salad and warm flatbreads.

Before roasting, the beef is smothered in a paste of spices, lemon and garlic, which penetrate the meat while it cooks. My vibrant salad of red onions and tomatoes, with loads of fresh coriander and parsley, and doused in lime juice and olive oil, acts as a side-kick to the beef. My twist on a traditional *raita* uses spinach stir-fried with garlic and mixed into the cooling yogurt, topped with toasted pine nuts. It's a heavenly combination. Just make sure you squeeze all the excess moisture out of the cooked spinach first. My favourite way to eat this meal is to stuff a flatbread with beef and salad, drizzle over plenty of *raita*, roll it all up and go for it!

FOR THE ROAST BEEF
600g/1lb 5oz beef fillet
4 garlic cloves
2 tsp paprika
2 tsp ground cumin
1 tsp ground coriander
2 tbsp olive oil
1 lemon
sea salt and freshly ground black
   pepper

FOR THE SPINACH RAITA
2 garlic cloves
2 tbsp olive oil
30g/1oz/scant ¼ cup pine nuts
200g/7oz baby spinach
225g/8oz/scant 1 cup Greek yogurt
1 lemon

**FOR THE ONION, TOMATO AND
   HERB SALAD**
2 red onions
1½ limes
2 large tomatoes
2 large handfuls of coriander
   leaves
2 large handfuls of parsley leaves
2 tbsp olive oil

TO SERVE
4 flatbreads

PREHEAT THE OVEN to 200°C/400°F/Gas 6 and take the beef out of the fridge to come to room temperature. Peel the garlic, then chuck it into a mini food processor, and add the paprika, cumin and ground coriander. Add the olive oil and a good pinch of salt and pepper. Squeeze in the juice from the lemon and blend until smooth.

PUT THE BEEF IN A ROASTING TIN, then tip over the paste and rub it all over the beef. Roast for 30–35 minutes until charred on the outside and beautifully tender on the inside.

WHILE THE BEEF COOKS, peel and slice the garlic for the raita. Heat the oil in a wok over a high heat and add the pine nuts. Stir-fry for 30 seconds until golden, then remove from the pan and leave to one side. Add the garlic to the pan. Stir-fry for 30 seconds until golden, then add the spinach and a pinch of salt. Continue to stir-fry for 2–3 minutes until the spinach has completely wilted. Tip the spinach into a fine sieve and leave to drain.

TO MAKE THE SALAD, peel and finely slice the red onions, then chuck them into a mixing bowl. Squeeze in the juice from the limes and add a good pinch of salt. Mix together and leave to one side.

USING THE BACK OF A SPOON, squeeze any excess moisture out of the spinach. Tip into a serving bowl and add the yogurt, then squeeze in the juice from the lemon and season with salt and pepper. Mix well, top with the pine nuts, then cover.

CUT THE TOMATOES for the salad in half and squeeze out the seeds, then finely chop the flesh and put it into the bowl with the onions. Finely chop the herbs and add them to the bowl. Pour over the oil and add a pinch of pepper. Mix well.

POP THE FLATBREADS into the oven for 2 minutes to warm through. When the beef is cooked, remove it from the oven and transfer it to a carving board. Slice the beef and serve it with the warm flatbreads, spinach raita and salad. Oh, and a glass or two of red.

Korean Steaks with Carrot Kimchi & Sanjim SERVES **4** READY IN **40 MINUTES**

FOR THE CARROT KIMCHI
1kg/2lb 4oz carrots
4 tbsp salt
2.5cm/1in piece fresh root ginger
1 garlic clove
1 tbsp fish sauce
2 tsp sugar
1 tsp chilli powder

3 tbsp yogurt
½ tsp clear honey
2 handfuls of chives

FOR THE SANJIM
1 garlic clove
12 spring onions
60g/2¼oz/½ cup walnuts
1 tbsp light soy sauce

2 tbsp chilli sauce
2 tsp clear honey
2 tsp sesame oil

FOR THE GRIDDLED STEAKS
2 tbsp olive oil
4 rib-eye steaks (about 250g/9oz each)
sea salt and freshly ground black pepper

TO MAKE THE KIMCHI, peel, then grate the carrots, using a food processor, and put them in a large mixing bowl. Add the salt and pour in 750ml/26fl oz/3 cups boiling water. Mix with a wooden spoon and leave to one side for 20 minutes. Meanwhile, make the dressing for the kimchi. Peel and grate the ginger into a serving bowl, then peel and crush in the garlic. Add the fish sauce, sugar, chilli powder, yogurt and honey. Finely chop the chives and add them to the bowl. Mix well, then cover and leave to one side.

TO MAKE THE SANJIM, peel the garlic and trim the spring onions, then chuck them both into a mini food processor, and add the walnuts. Blend into a coarse mix. Scoop into a serving bowl and add the soy sauce, chilli sauce, honey and sesame oil. Mix well, then cover and leave to one side.

TO COOK THE STEAKS, heat a griddle over a high heat until smoking. Rub the olive oil over the steaks and season both sides with salt and pepper. Griddle the steaks for 2–3 minutes on each side until brilliantly charred and perfectly pink in the centre. Remove from the heat and leave to one side to rest.

DRAIN AND RINSE THE CARROTS thoroughly under cold water. Repeat several times to remove all the salt. Squeeze out any excess water using your hands and add the carrots to the bowl with the dressing. Mix well and serve with the steaks and sanjim.

Essaouira Monkfish Tagine SERVES **4** READY IN **30 MINUTES**

600g/1lb 5oz monkfish fillet,
  membrane removed
½ lemon
150g/5½oz/heaped ¾ cup couscous
2 carrots
4 garlic cloves
2 red peppers

3 tbsp olive oil
2 tsp ground cumin
1 tsp paprika
½ tsp freshly ground black pepper
¼ tsp chilli powder
1 tsp sugar

400g/14oz/scant 1⅔ cups tinned
  chopped tomatoes
1 preserved lemon
30g/1oz/¼ cup pitted black olives
1 large handful of parsley leaves
sea salt

CUT THE MONKFISH into 2 pieces and put them in a mixing bowl. Squeeze over the juice from the lemon and add a pinch of salt. Mix together and leave to one side. Tip the couscous into a large mixing bowl and add 185ml/6fl oz/¾ cup warm water. Cover with cling film and leave for a minimum of 10 minutes, or until ready to eat.

PEEL THE CARROTS and garlic, and deseed the peppers, then finely slice them all. Heat the oil in a large saucepan over a high heat and add the peppers and carrots. Cook for 5–6 minutes, stirring occasionally, until they start to soften. Reduce the heat to medium and add the garlic, cumin, paprika, black pepper, chilli powder, sugar and a pinch of salt, and mix well.

TIP IN THE TOMATOES, pour over 200ml/7fl oz/scant 1 cup hot water and mix everything together really well. Bring to the boil and add the fish. Cover, leaving a small gap, and cook for 5–6 minutes. Turn the fish over, spoon some sauce over the top, then re-cover and cook for another 5–6 minutes until the fish is cooked through and tender.

WHILE THE FISH COOKS, remove the flesh from the preserved lemon and slice the skin into thin strips. Discard the flesh. Slice the olives and finely chop the parsley, then leave to one side. Fluff up the couscous with a fork. Chuck the preserved lemon skin, olives and parsley into the pan with the cooked fish, and mix well. To serve, cut the pieces of fish in half and serve with the couscous.

Phuket Snapper with Hoisin Noodles & Herb Salad SERVES **4** READY IN **40 MINUTES**

This delicious meal was inspired by our family holiday to Phuket a few years ago. I found hanging out and cooking with the superb chef, Jitty, at our villa way more interesting than spending a lazy afternoon by the pool. In her tiny, but immaculate, kitchen she would cook up a storm for every meal. She had trained in Bangkok and learnt about the regional cuisines of Thailand. Her repertoire of meals was incredible, and her use of flavour, colour and texture was spot on. I have borrowed a few elements from her glorious kitchen and added my own express twist to them so that you can get a Thai feast on the table in only 40 minutes.

The Worcestershire sauce is the secret ingredient in this dish, as used in Thailand. (I would have gone for fish sauce!) Worcestershire sauce adds a wicked flavour that most people won't recognize. It's strange that a British ingredient works so well with Thai flavours, but this is exactly why I love cooking – you can mix and match to create something sublime.

FOR THE ROASTED SNAPPER

1 tbsp groundnut oil, plus extra for greasing
2 red snapper (about 500g/1lb 2oz each), cleaned
2 lemongrass stalks
1 lime
5cm/2in piece fresh root ginger
1 tbsp Worcestershire sauce
1 tsp freshly ground black pepper
sea salt

FOR THE HERB SALAD

2 lemongrass stalks
2.5cm/1in piece fresh root ginger
½ red chilli
2 tbsp fish sauce
1½ tsp sugar
1 red onion
1½ limes
300g/10½oz carrots
2 large handfuls of coriander leaves
2 large handfuls of basil leaves
1 large handful of mint leaves
30g/1oz/scant ¼ cup peanuts

FOR THE HOISIN NOODLES

200g/7oz medium egg noodles
3 tbsp hoisin sauce
2 tbsp soy sauce
1 tbsp groundnut oil

PREHEAT THE OVEN to 200°C/400°F/Gas 6. Oil a piece of foil large enough to wrap up the fish, and put the snapper on top. Finely slice the lemongrass, lime and unpeeled ginger.

SPOON THE WORCESTERSHIRE SAUCE into the cavity of the fish and stuff with the lemongrass, lime and ginger, putting a few slices of lime on the top, if you like. Drizzle over the oil and sprinkle over the black pepper and a good pinch of salt. Wrap the fish tightly in the foil and put in a roasting tin. Roast the fish for 25–30 minutes until cooked through and tender.

MEANWHILE, MAKE THE SALAD. Remove the tough outer leaves of the lemongrass and cut off the ends of the stalks. Peel the ginger. Put the lemongrass into a mini food processor with the ginger, chilli, fish sauce and sugar, then blend into a smooth paste. Peel, then grate the onion into a large mixing bowl and squeeze over the juice from the limes. Mix well (this will help take the rawness out of the onions). Peel, then grate the carrots over the top.

FINELY CHOP MOST OF THE HERBS, reserving a few leaves to serve, and add to the bowl with the salad. Tip in the spice paste, toss together and transfer to a serving bowl. Cover and leave to one side.

COOK THE NOODLES in boiling water for 4–5 minutes until soft, or as directed on the packet. Drain and return to the pan. Pour over the hoisin sauce, soy sauce and oil. Mix everything together well and leave to one side. Scatter the peanuts and reserved herb leaves over the salad, and serve with the cooked fish and noodles.

Keralan Seafood Curry SERVES **4** READY IN **25 MINUTES**

250g/9oz/1¼ cups basmati rice
2.5cm/1in piece fresh root ginger
6 garlic cloves
1 green chilli
2 tsp ground coriander
½ tsp turmeric
250g/9oz/heaped 1¾ cups cherry
  tomatoes

2 tbsp groundnut oil
2 tsp black mustard seeds
2 large pinches of dried curry
  leaves
400ml/14fl oz/generous 1½ cups
  coconut milk
½ lime

250g/9oz boneless tilapia fillets
  or other white fish fillets
350g/12oz mixed seafood, such
  as squid rings, raw, peeled king
  prawns, shelled mussels
1 handful of coriander leaves
sea salt

COOK THE RICE in boiling water for 10–12 minutes until soft, or as directed on the packet. Drain and return to the pan. Cover the pan with a clean tea towel and then the lid. Leave to one side to allow the rice to fluff up.

MEANWHILE, PEEL THE GINGER AND GARLIC, and cut the top off the chilli, then put these ingredients into a mini food processor with the ground coriander, turmeric and a good pinch of salt. Blend into a smooth paste, adding a little water if necessary, and leave to one side.

CUT THE CHERRY TOMATOES in half and leave to one side. Heat the oil in a large saucepan over a medium heat and add the mustard seeds and curry leaves. Let them crackle for a few seconds, then tip in the spice paste. Stir-fry for 30 seconds, or until fragrant, then pour in the coconut milk. Squeeze in the juice from the lime and add a pinch of salt. Mix everything together really well and bring to the boil.

CHOP THE FISH into large, bite-sized pieces and add to the boiling sauce. Put the seafood and cherry tomatoes into the sauce and mix gently. Bring back to the boil, cover and reduce the heat to medium-low. Cook for 6–8 minutes, stirring occasionally, until all the seafood is cooked through and tender. Scatter the coriander over the cooked curry and serve with the rice.

Iain's Mighty Scallop Ceviche with Buckwheat Noodles & Avocado Salad SERVES **4** READY IN **30 MINUTES**

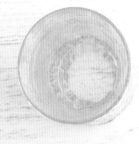

This is a super-fast, tangy and spicy South-east Asian-inspired dinner, with a bit of good old West London in there as well. Iain is one of my best friends, and he cooks a mean scallop. Ceviche is simply raw fish, or certain types of shellfish, that has been "cooked" in an acid, such as lime juice or vinegar. Make sure you buy the freshest seafood you can on the day you want to make the dish. If you want to reduce the chilli heat, remove the seeds – and if you like it to be a bit more piquant, chuck in an extra chilli.

FOR THE SCALLOP CEVICHE
30g/1oz/scant ¼ cup peanuts
2 lemongrass stalks
3 spring onions
1 red chilli
375g/13oz scallops
2 limes
2 tbsp fish sauce
1 tsp sugar
1 large handful of mint leaves

FOR THE BUCKWHEAT NOODLES
3 spring onions
200g/7oz buckwheat noodles
3 tbsp soy sauce
2 tbsp olive oil
1 tsp sesame oil

FOR THE AVOCADO SALAD
2 tbsp red wine vinegar
2 tsp sugar
2 tbsp olive oil
1 tsp sesame oil
1 tsp ground coriander
2 ripe avocados
1 tbsp pumpkin seeds
sea salt

ROUGHLY CHOP THE PEANUTS and put them in a frying pan. Toast the peanuts over a medium heat for 4–5 minutes, shaking the pan occasionally, until golden. Remove from the heat and leave to one side to cool.

MEANWHILE, REMOVE THE TOUGH outer leaves from the lemongrass and cut off the ends of the stalks. Trim all the spring onions for the ceviche and the noodles. Cut the top off the chilli, then finely chop half the chilli with 3 spring onions and the lemongrass, and put them into a bowl for the ceviche. Finely chop the remaining spring onions and chilli half, and put them in a separate small bowl to add to the noodles.

COOK THE NOODLES in boiling water for 5–7 minutes until soft, or as directed on the packet. While the noodles cook, cut the scallops into thin slices on the horizontal and lay them in an even layer in a shallow serving dish. Squeeze over the juice from the limes and shake the dish so that all the scallops are coated. Cover and leave to one side for 8–10 minutes so that the scallops can "cook" in the acid and turn slightly opaque in colour. Remember to shake the dish from time to time.

WHEN THE NOODLES HAVE COOKED, drain in a colander and refresh under cold water and drain again. Return them to the pan and dress with the soy sauce, olive oil and sesame oil. Mix well, then tip the noodles into a serving bowl. Scatter with the reserved chopped chilli and spring onions in the bowl for the noodles. Cover and leave to one side.

MAKE THE DRESSING for the salad by whisking the red wine vinegar and sugar together in a mixing bowl until the sugar dissolves. Pour in the olive oil and sesame oil, then add the coriander and a pinch of salt. Whisk everything together well.

CUT THE AVOCADOS in half and remove the stones with a knife. Scoop out small pieces of the flesh using a teaspoon and put them into the bowl with the dressing. Carefully mix everything together so that the avocado does not discolour. Tip the avocado on to a serving plate and scatter over the pumpkin seeds. Cover and leave to one side.

ADD THE FISH SAUCE to the "cooked" scallops, then add the sugar and the reserved chopped chilli, spring onions and lemongrass, and carefully toss together. Rip the mint leaves over the top, scatter over the toasted peanuts and serve with the noodles and avocado salad.

Panjim Clams with Coconut Okra SERVES **4** READY IN **30 MINUTES**

FOR THE CLAMS
1 onion
1 green chilli
2 tbsp groundnut oil
2 tsp garam masala
1 tsp turmeric
400ml/14fl oz/generous 1½ cups
  coconut cream
½ lime

1kg/2lb 4oz picked and cleaned
  clams
1 small handful of coriander leaves
sea salt

FOR THE COCONUT OKRA
350g/12oz okra
1 red onion
3 garlic cloves
1 green chilli

2 cardamom pods
2 tbsp groundnut oil
8 black peppercorns
185ml/6fl oz/¾ cup coconut cream
1 large pinch of dried curry leaves
20g/¾oz/scant ¼ cup raisins
½ lime

TO SERVE
4 small naan breads

PREHEAT THE OVEN to 180°C/350°F/Gas 4. Peel the onion and cut the top off the chilli. Finely chop both. Heat the oil in a saucepan over a medium heat and add both ingredients. Stir-fry for 4–5 minutes until just turning golden.

ADD THE GARAM MASALA and turmeric, mix well and pour in the coconut cream. Squeeze in the juice from the lime and add a good pinch of salt. Mix well, reduce the heat to low and simmer gently, stirring occasionally, while you start the okra.

CUT THE TOPS off the okra. Peel the red onion and garlic, and cut the top off the chilli, then finely chop the onion, garlic and chilli. Split the cardamom pods open by pressing down on them with the side of a knife. Heat the oil in a wok over a high heat and add the onion, garlic, chilli, cardamom and peppercorns. Stir-fry for 2–3 minutes until just golden, then add the okra and a good pinch of salt. Stir-fry for 2 minutes, then pour in the coconut cream. Add the curry leaves to the wok by rubbing them between your hands. Mix well, cover and reduce the heat to low. Cook for 5 minutes.

MEANWHILE, POP THE NAAN into the oven and switch it off, so that they just warm through. Add the raisins and the juice from the lime to the half-cooked okra, mix well, then cover and cook for 5 minutes, or until the okra is tender. While the okra finishes cooking, chuck the clams into the hot sauce, cover and cook for 4–5 minutes, shaking the pan occasionally, until the clams have opened. Discard any that remain closed. Chop the coriander and scatter it over the clams. Serve with the okra and naan.

Rooftop-Roasted Vegetables with Chilli Tapenade SERVES **4** READY IN **45 MINUTES**

**FOR THE ROOFTOP-
 ROASTED VEGETABLES**
2 red onions
2 red peppers
2 courgettes
1 aubergine
3 tbsp olive oil
1 tbsp dried thyme

250g/9oz/heaped 1¾ cups cherry
 tomatoes on the vine
1 loaf of fabulously crusty bread
55g/2oz/heaped ⅓ cup pine nuts
2 large handfuls of mint leaves
½ lemon
100g/3½oz feta cheese
sea salt and freshly ground black
 pepper

FOR THE CHILLI TAPENADE
1 garlic clove
85g/3oz/⅔ cup pitted black olives
4 anchovy fillets
1 large handful of parsley leaves
¼ tsp chilli powder
1½ tsp ground cumin
2 tbsp olive oil
½ lemon

PREHEAT THE OVEN to 200°C/400°F/Gas 6. Peel the onions and deseed the peppers, then cut the onions, peppers, courgettes and aubergine into large bite-sized pieces and put them in a roasting tin. Pour over the olive oil, then add the thyme and a good pinch of salt and pepper. Mix everything together really well and roast for 25 minutes, or until the vegetables are almost cooked through.

WHILE THE VEGETABLES ARE COOKING, make the chilli tapenade. Peel the garlic and put it into a blender or food processor. Add the olives, anchovies, parsley, chilli powder, cumin, oil and a pinch of salt and pepper. Squeeze in the juice from the lemon and blend into a coarse paste. Tip into a serving bowl, cover and leave to one side for the savoury flavours to develop.

WHEN THE VEGETABLES have almost cooked, remove from the oven and put the tomatoes over the top. Cook for another 8–10 minutes until all the vegetables are tender and golden and the tomatoes have just started to break down. Pop the bread into the oven for the last 5 minutes to warm through.

PUT THE PINE NUTS into a small frying pan over a medium heat and toast for 2–3 minutes, shaking the pan occasionally, until golden. Remove from the heat and leave to one side. Strip the mint leaves from the stems. Squeeze the juice of the lemon over the cooked vegetables, crumble over the feta cheese and rip over the mint. Scatter over the toasted pine nuts, then serve with the chilli tapenade and warm bread.

Sesame Aubergine Curry with Keralan Spinach & Sweetcorn Salad SERVES **4**   READY IN **45 MINUTES**

This vegetarian feast is my take on a classic North Indian curry. It's served with a fresh spinach and sweetcorn dish, hailing from Kerala, which is a cross between a side dish and a salad, and makes the perfect contrast. A lovely touch for maximum flavour when preparing this curry is to cut a slit in the aubergines and then to rub in a little of the spice mix. You can really taste the difference – the aubergines suck up all the flavour of the spices while they cook gently in the sauce.

FOR THE AUBERGINES
1 tbsp ground coriander
1 tbsp sesame seeds
½ tsp chilli powder
½ tbsp ground cumin
1½ tsp sea salt
350g/12oz baby aubergines
1 large red onion
2 tbsp groundnut oil
2.5cm/1in piece fresh root ginger
4 garlic cloves
3 tomatoes
a pinch of sugar

1 handful of coriander leaves
½ lemon

FOR THE RICE
250g/9oz/1¼ cups basmati rice

**FOR THE KERALAN SPINACH
   AND SWEETCORN SALAD**
1 tbsp groundnut oil
1 tsp cumin seeds
85g/3oz/heaped ½ cup cashew
   nuts
225g/8oz spinach

1 red onion
1 lemon
½ red chilli
140g/5oz/heaped ⅔ cup tinned
   sweetcorn
25g/1oz creamed coconut
sea salt

PUT THE GROUND CORIANDER, sesame seeds, chilli powder, ground cumin and salt into a spice grinder, and grind into a fine powder. Remove the stalks from the baby aubergines, if you like, and cut a slit about 2.5cm/1in deep into the opposite end. Rub a little of the ground spices into the slits – use about half the spices for this. Peel and finely chop the onion.

HEAT THE OIL in a saucepan over a medium heat and chuck in the onion. Cook for 4–5 minutes, stirring occasionally, until golden. While the onion cooks, peel the ginger and garlic, then finely chop the ginger, garlic and tomatoes. Add to the cooked onion and mix well. Add the remaining ground spices, the sugar and the prepared aubergines. Mix everything together really well, then cover and simmer for 20 minutes to allow the aubergines to cook through.

MEANWHILE, COOK THE RICE in boiling water for 10–12 minutes until soft, or as directed on the packet. Drain and return to the pan. Cover the pan with a clean tea towel and then the lid. Leave to one side so that the rice can fluff up.

MAKE THE SALAD while the rice cooks. Heat the oil in a wok over a medium heat and add the cumin seeds and cashew nuts. Stir-fry for 45 seconds, then add the spinach and a pinch of salt. Continue to stir-fry for 2–3 minutes until the spinach has completely wilted. Remove from the heat and leave to one side.

PEEL AND FINELY CHOP THE ONION, and put it in a mixing bowl. Squeeze over the juice from the lemon, add a pinch of salt and mix well. Finely chop the chilli and add it to the same bowl. Drain the sweetcorn and tip it into the bowl, then add the cooked spinach, making sure you scrape all the oil and cumin into the mixing bowl. Mix everything together really well and transfer to a serving bowl. Grate the coconut over the top, then cover and leave to one side.

WHEN THE AUBERGINES HAVE COOKED, remove the lid from the pan and cook for 5 minutes, stirring occasionally, to allow the sauce to thicken. Roughly tear up the coriander. Scatter the coriander over the cooked curry and squeeze over the juice from the lemon. Serve with the cooked rice and the colourful salad.

NAUGHTY BUT NICE

The name says it all really. This chapter is packed with delicious desserts, fabulous drinks and killer cocktails that can all be made so fast you might as well make two at a time! Even the longest recipe takes only 30 minutes from start to finish. My Mint Tea & Lemongrass Martini takes less than 10 minutes to make and will get any party started. My Salted Caramel Chocolate Sauce – which is quite simply the greatest sauce there ever was and ever will be – poured generously over vanilla ice cream, takes only 10 minutes to make and will win you a legion of fans with every serving. My beautiful, sticky Kika Cakes flavoured with almonds and vanilla, and served with an Orange & Ginger Glaze, take only 25 minutes to make, proving that there is even time for a bit of gentle baking.

Vanilla Ice Cream with Salted Caramel Chocolate Sauce SERVES **4** READY IN **10 MINUTES**

This is probably the best sauce ever! A bold statement, I know, but what could be better than a wickedly sweet salted caramel sauce, loaded up with rich dark chocolate and served warm and oozing over vanilla ice cream? Find an especially good vanilla ice cream to do the sauce justice.

FOR THE ICE CREAM
500ml/17fl oz tub of awesome
   vanilla ice cream
40g/1½oz/⅓ cup hazelnuts

FOR THE SALTED CARAMEL
   CHOCOLATE SAUCE
125g/4½oz/⅔ cup light brown
   sugar
60g/2¼oz butter
50ml/1¾fl oz/scant ¼ cup
   double cream
100g/3½oz dark chocolate
   (85% cocoa solids)
sea salt

TAKE THE VANILLA ICE CREAM out of the freezer to soften. Meanwhile, tip the sugar for the sauce into a saucepan and add 1½ tablespoons water. Bring to the boil over a high heat and cook for 2–3 minutes, shaking the pan occasionally, until all the sugar has dissolved. Roughly chop the nuts while the sugar dissolves.

REMOVE THE PAN from the heat and add the butter. Return the pan to a low heat and melt the butter, whisking continuously. Continue to whisk for another 1 minute, or until the caramel turns light brown. Add a good pinch of salt and whisk well. Pour in the cream and continue to whisk until velvety smooth.

BREAK UP THE CHOCOLATE into the sauce and whisk continuously until completely melted and the sauce has thickened a little. Carefully pour the sauce into a heatproof jug and serve immediately with the ice cream and the hazelnuts to sprinkle over the top.

Goan Explosion Truffles SERVES 4   READY IN 30 MINUTES

Actual truffles in 30 minutes – get in! The trick is to get your cake tin really cold and make sure that the truffle mix goes into it in a thin layer so that it sets really fast. Scoop out the truffle mix with a teaspoon or a fancy melon baller and drop each ball into the ground pistachio nuts for a speedy coating. Coffee, cardamom and chilli funk up these truffles. Use the maddest, greenest pistachios you can find to get the perfect Goan experience.

1 handful of ice cubes
100ml/3½fl oz/generous ⅓ cup
  double cream
15g/½oz butter

100g/3½oz dark chocolate (70%
  cocoa solids)
¼ tsp espresso powder
¼ tsp ground cardamom

a pinch of chilli powder
55g/2oz/heaped ⅓ cup shelled
  green pistachio nuts

PUT THE ICE in a 25cm/10in cake tin with a fixed base and pop it into the freezer. Pour the cream into a small saucepan and add the butter. Cook over a medium heat for 2–3 minutes, stirring occasionally, until the butter melts.

MEANWHILE, BREAK UP THE CHOCOLATE into a microwaveproof bowl. Put it into the microwave and heat for 1 minute on high, or until the chocolate just starts to melt. (Alternatively, melt the chocolate in a heatproof bowl over a pan of gently simmering water, making sure the base of the bowl doesn't touch the water.) Remove the bowl from the microwave or steamer and add the espresso powder, cardamom and chilli powder. Pour over the hot cream and whisk together until thick and smooth.

WORKING AS FAST AS YOU CAN, take the cake tin out of the freezer, discard the ice and wipe the tin dry with some kitchen paper. Pour the chocolate mixture into the tin and spread it out evenly in a thin layer, no deeper than 5mm/¼in, otherwise it won't set in time. Put the cake tin into the freezer and freeze for 20 minutes, or until set.

CHUCK THE NUTS into a food processor and blend into a coarse rubble. Tip into a mixing bowl. Using a teaspoon or melon baller, scoop out the truffle mixture and drop each truffle ball into the bowl of crushed nuts and give the bowl a shake. Make sure all the truffles are coated, then tip into a serving bowl and serve.

Pineapple & Lime Pie SERVES **4** READY IN **20 MINUTES**

Right now, I am in love with America, and this pudding was inspired by the American classic, key lime pie. I have used pineapple, with a hint of chilli, instead of the traditional lime, plus a no-bake biscuit base to make it quick.

110g/3¾oz butter
½ pineapple
30g/1oz demerara sugar
a pinch of crushed chilli flakes
140g/5oz digestive biscuits

400ml/14fl oz/generous 1½ cups
  double cream
2 tbsp icing sugar
½ lime

PUT 80G/2¾OZ OF THE BUTTER in a small saucepan over a medium heat and the remaining butter in a small frying pan over a medium heat.

WHILE THE BUTTER MELTS, cut the top and bottom off the pineapple, then stand it upright on your chopping board. Slice off the skin, cutting downwards from top to bottom. Carefully cut out any pieces of skin left on the fruit. Cut the pineapple half in half lengthways, then slice off the woody core so that you are left with the soft fruit. Cut the pineapple flesh into small pieces and add them to the small frying pan. Add the demerara sugar and a pinch of chilli flakes. Mix well and cook for 8–10 minutes, shaking the pan occasionally, until the pineapple starts to soften and the sauce has thickened. Remove from the heat and leave to one side to cool a little.

PUT THE BISCUITS into a food processor and blend into a fine powder while the pineapple cooks. Tip into a mixing bowl and pour over the melted butter from the small saucepan. Mix well. Line the base and sides of a 19cm/7½in springform cake tin with baking parchment and press the biscuit mix into the base, using the back of a spoon. Put the cake tin into the fridge to chill while you whisk the cream.

POUR THE CREAM into a large mixing bowl and add the icing sugar. Zest in the lime, squeeze in the juice, then whisk into firm peaks. Remove the cake tin from the fridge and fill with the cream. Top with the pineapple pieces, drizzle over the sauce from the pineapple, then open the side of the cake tin, remove the paper and serve.

Mango & Vanilla Coconut Pots SERVES **4** READY IN **10 MINUTES**

Coconut and mango are best mates and appear in various guises in Southeast Asian desserts. These fresh little puddings are inspired by the many varieties I have eaten over the years. I have made my version to be as quick as possible without cutting back on any flavour. The mango is squished together with sugar and orange to soften it and intensify the taste. The sweet fruit is then topped off with luscious cream that has been whipped with coconut cream to add that authentic Asian twist.

2 ripe mangoes
4 tbsp icing sugar
½ orange
300ml/10½fl oz/scant 1¼ cups
  double cream

70ml/2¼fl oz/generous ¼ cup
  coconut cream
1 tsp vanilla extract

CUT OFF THE MANGO PEEL, then slice off the flesh from the sides and around the stone. Chop into bite-sized pieces, then put them in a mixing bowl.

ADD HALF THE ICING SUGAR and squeeze in the juice from the orange. Mix together using your hands to slightly break up the mango, then leave to one side.

POUR THE DOUBLE CREAM into a mixing bowl and whisk into firm peaks. Add the coconut cream, remaining icing sugar and the vanilla extract, and whisk together. To serve, divide the mango mixture into four glasses and top each one with the cream.

Pumpkin, Chocolate & Walnut Puddings SERVES **4** READY IN **25 MINUTES**

This is my version of a classic Turkish dessert of slow-braised pumpkin served with walnuts. My twist is to add chunks of bitter dark chocolate, which melt into the sweet pumpkin, topped with lovely soft whipped cream.

750g/1lb 10oz pumpkin
125ml/4fl oz/½ cup double cream
25g/1oz butter
55g/2oz/¼ cup demerara sugar

6 cloves
25g/1oz dark chocolate (70% cocoa solids)
55g/2oz/scant ½ cup walnuts

PEEL AND DESEED THE PUMPKIN and cut it into 2.5cm/1in pieces. Chuck them into a microwaveproof bowl and add 100ml/3½fl oz/generous ⅓ cup water. Cover with cling film and microwave on high for 10 minutes, or until the pieces are soft but haven't turned to mush. To check, poke them with a sharp knife – it should slide out very easily.

WHIP THE CREAM to soft peaks while the pumpkin cooks, and leave to one side. Put the butter, sugar and cloves in a frying pan, and heat over a low heat. Once the sugar starts to look a bit dry, shake the pan and it will suddenly dissolve into a liquid. Once completely dissolved, remove from the heat – it will look as though it has split from the butter, but don't worry, I promise this is how it's meant to look.

CUT TWO-THIRDS OF THE CHOCOLATE into tiny pieces and divide into 4 portions. Scrunch the walnuts between your hands over a bowl so that they break up into small pieces.

USING A SLOTTED SPOON, carefully transfer the cooked pumpkin to the frying pan with the sugar mixture. Cook over a low heat for 5 minutes, stirring occasionally.

ADD ALL BUT 1 TABLESPOON of the crushed walnuts to the pumpkin and mix everything together. Spoon the pumpkin into four heatproof glasses, picking out the cloves as you go. Scatter a pile of chocolate over each one and spoon over a quarter of the cream. Sprinkle over the remaining walnuts and grate the last of the chocolate over the top. Serve immediately, so that the chocolate oozes through the pudding.

Luang Prabang Coconut Rice Pudding SERVES **4**   READY IN **20 MINUTES**

This is my express version of the classic Lao pudding. Instead of using Lao red rice and steaming it for ages, I use jasmine rice, which I parboil, then it's finished off in coconut milk, sugar and cardamom. A good grating of nutmeg, plus some sesame seeds, fresh mango and mint leaves provide a contrast of different flavours, colours and textures to the creamy rice.

115g/4oz/heaped ½ cup jasmine rice
200ml/7fl oz/scant 1 cup coconut milk
40g/1½oz/scant ¼ cup caster sugar

¼ nutmeg
3 cardamom pods
2 tbsp sesame seeds
1 large mango
1 handful of mint leaves

COOK THE RICE in boiling water for 8 minutes. Meanwhile, pour the coconut milk into a saucepan. Add the sugar and grate in the nutmeg. Crush the cardamom pods by pressing down with the side of a knife, then put them into the coconut milk. Mix well and bring to the boil over a medium heat. Reduce the heat to low and simmer gently while the rice is cooking. Drain the rice and leave in the colander.

MEANWHILE, PUT THE SESAME SEEDS in a frying pan and toast over a medium heat for 2–3 minutes, shaking the pan continuously, until golden. Remove from the heat and leave to one side.

TIP THE COOKED RICE into the coconut milk and mix well. Cover and cook gently for 5 minutes. Remove the lid and cook for another 1 minute, stirring continuously, to thicken. The rice should have the consistency of a lovely oozy risotto. Remove the cardamom if you prefer.

CUT OFF THE MANGO PEEL while the rice finishes cooking, then slice off the flesh from the sides and around the stone, and chop into bite-sized pieces. Divide the rice into four serving bowls and top each bowl with pieces of mango. Scatter over the sesame seeds and mint leaves, and serve.

Kika Cakes with Orange & Ginger Glaze MAKES **10 SMALL CAKES** READY IN **25 MINUTES**

Express cooking even means baking. Vanilla, orange and almonds make the base of my spongy cakes, which soak up the yummy marmalade and ginger glaze. I prefer to use a slightly sweet marmalade to make my glaze, so the cakes take on that flavour as well.

1 egg
150g/5½oz/heaped ⅔ cup caster
  sugar, plus 1 tbsp for the glaze
1 orange

2 tsp vanilla extract
120g/4¼oz/scant 1¼ cups fine
  ground almonds
120g/4¼oz/scant 1 cup plain flour

¾ tsp baking powder
150g/5½oz/scant ½ cup
  marmalade
¼ tsp ground ginger

PREHEAT THE OVEN to 200°C/400°F/Gas 6. Crack the egg into a large mixing bowl and add the 150g/5½oz/heaped ⅔ cup sugar. Whisk the egg and sugar together until fluffy and light. Zest the whole orange into the bowl and squeeze in the juice from one half. Add the vanilla extract and ground almonds, then sift over the flour and baking powder. Gently fold everything together to make a thick batter.

LINE 10 MUFFIN CUPS with paper cases. Scoop the batter into each of the cases – each case will hold about 3 tablespoons of batter. Bake for 12–14 minutes until golden on the top and cooked in the centre – a skewer inserted into the centre should come out clean.

WHILE THE CAKES COOK, put the marmalade, ginger and the 1 tablespoon sugar into a small non-stick saucepan. Squeeze the juice from the remaining orange half into the pan and bring to the boil over a medium-low heat, stirring occasionally, until the glaze ingredients dissolve together.

REMOVE THE CAKES from the oven and top each one with the hot glaze. Leave to one side to cool for a couple of minutes, then serve while still warm.

Cinnamon Fig Tarts SERVES **4** READY IN **25 MINUTES**

Figs are a staple element of desserts across the Middle East, adding colour, flavour and texture, and they work beautifully with spices. I have often seen the humble fig transformed into a spectacular dish, and it's perfect for a quick dessert. Baking figs intensifies their flavour, so I've laid them on puff pastry that was sprinkled with demerara sugar, cinnamon and ground ginger. When cooked, they become wrapped in a wonderful, sweet, warm blanket. The clementine and mint cream freshens up the flavours and accentuates the warmth of the spices.

flour, for dusting
150g/5½oz puff pastry, defrosted
  if frozen
1 tsp demerara sugar

½ tsp ground cinnamon
¼ tsp ground ginger
6 small or 3 medium figs
250ml/9fl oz/1 cup double cream

2 clementines
2 tbsp icing sugar
1 small handful of mint leaves

PREHEAT THE OVEN to 200°C/400°F/Gas 6. Line a baking sheet with baking parchment. Scrunch it up in your hands and smooth it out to stop it rolling up.

FLOUR THE WORK SURFACE and roll out the pastry to just under 5mm/¼in thick. Cut the pastry into 4 rectangles, measuring 10 × 15cm/4 × 6in, and put them on to the baking parchment. Prick each one a few times with a fork.

MIX THE DEMERARA SUGAR, cinnamon and ginger in a bowl, then sprinkle evenly over each pastry. Cut the small figs in half, or the medium figs into quarters, and put 3 pieces of fig down the centre of each rectangle. Bake the tarts for 18–20 minutes until puffed and golden.

MEANWHILE, POUR THE CREAM into a large mixing bowl. Zest in of 1 of the clementines and squeeze in the juice of both. Sift in the icing sugar, then whip the cream until it forms soft peaks. Save a few mint leaves for decoration and finely chop the remainder. Fold the chopped mint leaves into the cream. Serve the hot tarts with a large dollop of the cream and a scattering of mint leaves.

Strawberry Layer Cakes SERVES **4** READY IN **25 MINUTES**

These awesome crispy, creamy strawberry layer cakes are a nod to my time in Morocco. Cinnamon, orange and vanilla add the exotic flavours and turn this dessert into something out of the ordinary.

350g/12oz/2⅓ cups strawberries
½ tsp ground cinnamon, plus a
    little extra for dusting
3 tbsp icing sugar
½ orange

2 large sheets of filo pastry,
    defrosted if frozen
300g/10½oz/scant 1¼ cups full-fat
    Greek yogurt
1 tsp vanilla extract
55g/2oz/scant ½ cup walnut pieces

SLICE THE STRAWBERRIES, discarding their tops, and put them in a shallow dish. Sprinkle over the cinnamon and 1 tablespoon of the icing sugar. Squeeze over the juice from the orange and mix well. Cover and leave to one side.

CUT THE FILO PASTRY into 12 rectangles, each measuring 8 × 12cm/3¼ × 4½in (and cover the filo with a damp tea towel to prevent it from drying out). Heat a large frying pan over a medium-high heat and pan-fry the filo pastry in batches until golden and crispy. This will take about 1–1½ minutes on one side and 30 seconds–1 minute on the other. Remove from the pan and put carefully to one side.

PUT THE YOGURT in a mixing bowl while cooking the filo, and add the remaining icing sugar and the vanilla. Whisk everything together well and leave to one side.

WHEN ALL THE FILO IS COOKED you can construct the cakes. Put a piece of cooked filo on to a serving plate and add a spoonful of yogurt on top. Spread it out and cover with a thin layer of strawberries. Put another piece of filo over the strawberries, and then repeat with more yogurt and another layer of strawberries. Put a third piece of filo over the strawberries, spread a spoonful of yogurt over the top, then break up some of the walnuts and scatter them over. Add a pinch of cinnamon, then repeat for the other 3 layer cakes. Serve with any remaining strawberries.

TINY TOWNS, CANTO POP & SHENYANG BANANAS

Shenyang is a town in north-eastern China, nestled near the borders of Mongolia and North Korea. It gets very cold, the people are unusually tall and the food is out of this world. By Chinese standards it's considered a small town – by mine it was massive. The "tiny town" of Shenyang consisted of around 8 million people, a plethora of Italian designer stores, underground shopping malls and incredible food everywhere.

It wasn't just very cold in Shenyang when I went – it was completely freezing! Minus 3 during the daytime, without windchill, to be exact. Being that cold meant that having a wander was a very hard thing to do. When I did stroll around it was fairly bleak, until I was ushered through what looked like a subway entrance. Bam! There it was – the high street. It was underground, so you could walk around without freezing to death. This was no ordinary high street, though. The shops selling the big brands were at street level, but this was London's Camden Market of high streets – neon lit, pulsating to the sound of canto pop and Chinese techno, and filled with uber-cool kids decked out in Hello Kitty and glasses without any lenses.

There was street food everywhere – day-glo hot dogs and kebabs, duck heads and tongues, pancakes and rice buns, mashed potatoes and soups, noodles and salads, fruit and amazing battered bananas, which were skewered on a stick and covered in syrup and crunchy sesame seeds. They were delicious and the perfect sugar hit for such cold weather.

Shenyang Bananas with Honey & Sesame Seeds SERVES **4** READY IN **15 MINUTES**

I have created a really quick version of the tasty snack from that underground high street in Shenyang. Sesame seeds and flour form the base of a batter to coat the bananas, and it's flavoured with warming ground cloves and chilli powder. The flavour of the spices lingers when the bananas are cooked, and it's somehow exaggerated by the runny honey drizzled over before serving. This is express cooking at its best.

sunflower oil, for shallow-frying
150g/5½oz/scant 1¼ cups plain
  flour
2 tbsp icing sugar
¾ tsp ground cloves
¾ tsp chilli powder

55g/2oz/heaped ⅓ cup sesame
  seeds
1 egg
2 bananas
3 tbsp clear honey

POUR THE OIL into a saucepan to a depth of 1.5cm/⅝in and heat over a medium-high heat. Meanwhile, sift the flour, icing sugar, cloves and chilli powder into a large mixing bowl, and add 30g/1oz/scant ¼ cup of the sesame seeds. Crack in the egg, then slowly whisk in 200ml/7fl oz/scant 1 cup cold water to form a smooth batter.

PEEL THE BANANAS and cut them into 1cm/½in pieces. Put the pieces into the batter and carefully transfer them to the hot oil using a pair of tongs. Fry the bananas for 30–45 seconds on each side until beautifully golden and crispy.

REMOVE THE BANANAS from the pan and put them on kitchen paper to drain. Transfer the bananas to a serving plate and drizzle over the honey. Scatter over the remaining sesame seeds and serve.

Mint Tea & Lemongrass Martini SERVES **4** READY IN **10 MINUTES**

Martinis are cool. Fact. We have all seen *Mad Men*! A classic martini still eludes me, though. It's a bit like drinking rocket fuel, so I always go for a flavoured one. For my express martini, I take advantage of the clean taste of vodka and add some lovely flavours – green tea, lemongrass and mint. Adding honey and lemongrass to the green tea while it brews means that all the flavours infuse in just a couple of minutes. What you get is an instant, flavoured sugar syrup – and that means a very quick martini.

2 lemongrass stalks
1 green tea bag
3 tbsp clear honey
2 handfuls of ice

1 handful of mint leaves, plus a few
   extra leaves to serve
200ml/7fl oz/scant 1 cup vodka
1 lime

BASH EACH LEMONGRASS STALK to break it up, and roughly chop it into 2.5cm/1in pieces. Chuck the lemongrass into a jug or cocktail shaker and add the tea bag, honey and 200ml/7fl oz/scant 1 cup boiling water. Mix well and leave to infuse for 3 minutes.

MEANWHILE, PUT A FEW ICE CUBES into four martini glasses and leave to chill. Remove the tea bag from the syrup and add the mint. Pour in the vodka and squeeze in the juice from the lime. Chuck in a large handful of ice and mix together really well.

TIP THE ICE OUT of the martini glasses and strain in the mint tea and lemongrass martini. Add a few mint leaves and serve.

Burnt Lemon & Vanilla Tequila Shots

SERVES **4**   READY IN **10 MINUTES**

I love tequila, real tequila – one that is golden and made from 100 per cent agave. This means the drink is smooth and well rounded, not like horrid paint stripper in a bottle, with a funny Mexican-hat lid and perhaps a rank insect festering at the bottom. When you work with great tequila it's important not to mess with it too much. The vanilla in my shots accentuates the flavour of the tequila, and the burnt lemon adds to the already smoky taste of the drink. It needs balance and therefore sweetness. In an ideal world, use an agave syrup. But, failing that, a really great runny honey will work just as well.

2 lemons
1 tsp olive oil
200ml/7fl oz/scant 1 cup 100% agave light tequila

2 tbsp agave syrup or clear honey
1 tsp vanilla extract
2 handfuls of ice

CUT THE LEMONS in half and brush the flesh with a little oil. Put the lemons, cut-side down, into a non-stick frying pan. Heat over a medium heat and cook for 4–4½ minutes until the lemons are turning from a golden colour to just charred. Remove the pan from the heat and leave to one side.

POUR THE TEQUILA into a small mixing jug or cocktail shaker and add the agave syrup and vanilla extract. Carefully squeeze the lemons into the jug and run a teaspoon around the flesh side to get all the sticky pieces out. Add the ice and mix well. Pour into four long shot glasses and serve immediately – *Salud*!

Hot & Spicy Bourbon SERVES **4**   READY IN **5 MINUTES**

Bourbon has been my drink of the month for quite some time now. It has a good smoky flavour that comes from the charred oak barrels it is aged in. The hot, sticky Kentucky air speeds up this ageing process, so the bourbon ends up being a relatively young drink. This gives it a beautifully smooth and mellow taste. As you can tell, I am quite into it! In this delicious hot drink the star anise, cinnamon and cloves accentuate the taste of the bourbon, and the orange and honey provide the classic accompanying flavours. This is advanced hot-toddy drinking, people!

4 star anise
4 cinnamon sticks
8 cloves

1 orange
250ml/9fl oz/1 cup bourbon
4 tbsp clear honey

BOIL THE KETTLE. Meanwhile, divide the star anise, cinnamon sticks and cloves into four mugs.

USING A PEELER, peel 4 strips of orange zest, give them a twist and add them to the mugs. Slice 4 slices from the orange and put one in each mug.

DIVIDE THE BOURBON and honey into the mugs, then fill each one to the top with boiling water. Stir each mug of hot and spicy bourbon with a cinnamon stick and serve.

INDEX

Acknowledgements

THANK YOU TO: Annie and Mike; Lizzie and Amish; Little South Island BBQ for the inspiration and good times; Heather at Villa Dinari; my godson Max; Duncan Baird Publishers for doing it again; Rita and family in Goa; Gail in Fez; my brother Tom and his gorgeous wife Rach, for always putting me up.

Picture Credits